Public Relations as Public Diplomacy

This is a study of the Royal Bank of Canada's *Monthly Letter*, which was initially created in 1920 as a traditional economic newsletter and later evolved quite serendipitously into a publication marvel when, in 1943, it came under the influence of John Heron, journalist and publicist, gaining mass appeal both domestically and abroad.

This concise history documents the inception, development and rise to popularity of the *Monthly Letter*, telling the untold story of how a corporate newsletter became a tool of international public diplomacy. The purpose of this writing is to demonstrate the entanglement of the fields of public diplomacy and public relations and to offer a more palatable conceptualization of them as two discrete, but necessary, parts of a whole. It acknowledges the varied soup of contested terminology which surrounds the field of public diplomacy (e.g. corporate diplomacy, cultural diplomacy and economic diplomacy). This work conceptualizes public diplomacy and public relations as two parts of a whole in which the sum is greater than its individual parts, juxtaposing the two fields in relation to one another, diminishing neither.

The contents of this work provide a broad overview of the fields of public diplomacy and public relations that could serve as an introduction and discussion point for students and scholars in both fields and offers a specific case study around which lively discussion and additional study can ensue.

Sandra L. Braun is Associate Professor of Public Relations at Mount Royal University in Calgary, Alberta, Canada.

Routledge Insights in Public Relations Research

The field of PR research has grown exponentially in recent years and academics at all career levels are seeking authoritative publication opportunities for their scholarship. **Routledge Insights in PR Research** is a new program of short-form book publications, presenting key topics across the discipline and their foundation in research. This series will provide a forward-facing global forum for new and emerging research topics which critically evaluate contemporary PR thinking and practice.

This format is particularly effective for introducing new scholarship reflecting the diverse range of research approaches and topics in the field. It is particularly effective for:

- Overview of an emerging area or "hot topic."
- In-depth case-study.
- Tailored research-based information for a practitioner readership.
- Update of a research paper to reflect new findings or wider perspectives.
- Exploration of analytical or theoretical innovations.
- Topical response to current affairs or policy debates.

Authors from practice and the academy will be able to quickly pass on their thinking and findings to fellow PR scholars, researchers, MA and PhD students and informed practitioners.

Strategic Communication for Startups and Entrepreneurs in China
Linjuan Rita Men, Yi Grace Ji and Zifei Fay Chen

Public Relations as Public Diplomacy
The Royal Bank of Canada's *Monthly Letter*, 1943–2003
Sandra L. Braun

For more information about this series, please visit www.routledge.com/Routledge-Insights-in-Public-Relations-Research/book-series/RIPRR

Public Relations as Public Diplomacy

The Royal Bank of Canada's
Monthly Letter, 1943–2003

Sandra L. Braun

Routledge
Taylor & Francis Group

LONDON AND NEW YORK

First published 2020 by Routledge

2 Park Square, Milton Park, Abingdon, Oxon OX14 4RN
605 Third Avenue, New York, NY 10017

Routledge is an imprint of the Taylor & Francis Group, an informa business

First issud in paperback 2021

British Library Cataloguing-in-Publication Data
A catalogue record for this book is available from the British Library

Library of Congress Cataloging-in-Publication Data
Names: Braun, Sandra L., author.
Title: Public relations as public diplomacy : the Royal Bank of Canada's
    monthly letter, 1943–2003 / Sandra L. Braun.
Description: First Edition. | New York : Routledge, 2020. |
    Series: Routledge insights in public relations research |
    Includes bibliographical references and index.
Identifiers: LCCN 2019052813 (print) | LCCN 2019052814 (ebook)
Subjects: LCSH: Royal Bank of Canada. | Banks and banking—Canada. |
    Public relations—Canada.
Classification: LCC HG2708.R69 B74 2020 (print) |
    LCC HG2708.R69 (ebook) | DDC 659.2/633210971—dc23
LC record available at https://lccn.loc.gov/2019052813
LC ebook record available at https://lccn.loc.gov/2019052814

ISBN: 978-0-367-33974-6 (hbk)
ISBN: 978-1-03-217524-9 (pbk)
DOI: 10.4324/9780429323256

Typeset in Times New Roman
by Apex CoVantage, LLC

Contents

Preface

This is a case study examining the intersection of public relations and public diplomacy.

Scholars have called for more empirical study, including case studies, to investigate and build theory at the intersection of public relations and public diplomacy (Bouzanis, 2009; Vanc & Fitzpatrick, 2016). This is in response.

This is an historical case study of the Royal Bank of Canada (RBC) and its publication *The Monthly Letter* (heretofore referred to as *The Letter*) from 1943–2003. Begun as a staid, typical bank newsletter of its day, it came under the influence of a publicist and journalist, John Heron, who turned it into a lively, engaging, human-interest public relations tool for the bank. The new format captured the imaginations of RBC customers at home and abroad as the bank engaged in global expansion. The purpose of this treatise is to examine the publication, not only as a public relations tool but also as a tool of public diplomacy, corporate diplomacy, economic diplomacy and cultural diplomacy, illustrating, as a case in point, the fine distinctions between the fields of public diplomacy and public relations and the need for a definition and conceptualization of public diplomacy as intricately intertwined with its communication processes.

Case studies are valuable because they "are a means of extending and fine tuning [theories] by holding them accountable to concrete experience" (Lowes, 2002, p. 123). Case studies give us practical examples to study and provide comparative information with a view of practice.

The case study is an excellent method for theory building and generating hypotheses and has been said to hold the potential to "produce the best theory" (Walton, 1992, p. 129). Case studies are also ideal to assist with falsification, a point of scientific rigour as promoted by Karl Popper (1959); if one case does not fit the proposition, then the proposition must be changed.

Flyvbjerg (2006) challenges the belief that case studies are not valuable because they cannot be generalized:

> One can often generalize on the basis of a single case, and the case study may be central to scientific development via generalization as supplement or alternative to other methods. But formal generalization is overvalued as a source of scientific development, whereas 'the force of example' is underestimated.
>
> (p. 12)

Cases are intriguing because the information each one holds can be quite varied and even unique – some cases can tell us very little, while others might be quite representative, but they all tell us something. Extreme cases can be quite informative for telling us what is not the norm (Flyvbjerg, 2006). In other words, each case is valuable and comes with its unique DNA; it is a researcher's delight to unravel it. I like this view of case studies because it reinforces the potential value inherent in each case and encourages a healthy amount of scholarly activity into one case or across a variety of cases. There is value in all pathways to knowledge: "The case study is a necessary and sufficient method for certain important research tasks in the social sciences, and it is a method that holds up well when compared to other methods in the gamut of social science research methodology" (Flyvbjerg, 2006, p. 26).

Cases are qualitative approaches rich with detail, complexities and sometimes ambiguity; therefore, they come with "a substantial element of narrative" (Flyvbjerg, 2006, p. 21; Mitchell & Charmaz, 1996). This complexity adds to their realism and richness. It also signals caution in providing hard summaries and making overly simplistic conclusions. This case comes with a good deal of narrative which tells a story, sets the case into its historical context and attempts to make reasonable interpretation.

Case studies are also intriguing for their implication across domains (Flyvbjerg, 2006). This is certainly the hope here as we investigate the intersection of public relations and public diplomacy.

This particular case study is historical in nature. Primary sources were the online archives of RBC, where digitized copies of *The Letter* from 1943–2008 are housed, totaling some 500 back issues. This information was contextualized and supplemented with a study of relevant secondary historical literature, including the history of RBC, an examination of social, political and economic trends, all the while examining for the dynamics at the intersection of public diplomacy and public relations. The period 1943 to 2003 was selected because December 1943 represents the first issue penned by

John Heron, under whose editorship *The Letter* became both a publishing marvel and diplomatic curiosity; it is also the earliest issue available in the online archive. The year 2003 serves as an endpoint to the study because it is the final issue of Heron's successor, Robert Stewart, who continued Heron's work in similar fashion; however, this examination is focused on relevant key periods and topics in a thematic approach.

This treatise will reinforce the fine distinctions between the fields of public relations and public diplomacy and illustrate the criticality of the communication function of public diplomacy, necessitating a re-examination of definitions, which this work also puts forward.

Part I

Background

1 Public diplomacy and public relations

Two parts of a whole

The Blind Men and the Elephant by John Godfrey Saxe

It was six men of Indostan,
To learning much inclined,
Who went to see the elephant
(Though all of them were blind),
That each by observation
Might satisfy his mind.

The first approached the elephant,
And happening to fall
Against his broad and sturdy side,
At once began to bawl:
"God bless me! But the elephant
Is very like a wall!"

The second, feeling of the tusk,
Cried, "Ho! What have we here
So very round and smooth and sharp?
To me 'tis mighty clear,
This wonder of an elephant
Is very like a spear!"

The third approached the animal,
And happening to take
The squirming trunk within his hands,
Thus boldly up and spake:
"I see," quoth he, "the elephant
Is very like a snake!"

The fourth reached out an eager hand,
And felt about the knee:
"What most this wondrous beast is like
Is mighty plain," quoth he,
" 'Tis clear enough the elephant
Is very like a tree!"

The fifth, who chanced to touch the ear,
Said "E'en the blindest man
Can tell what this resembles most;
Deny the fact who can,
This marvel of an elephant
Is very like a fan!"

The sixth no sooner had begun
About the beast to grope,
Then, seizing on the swinging tail
That fell within his scope,
"I see," quoth he, "the elephant
Is very like a rope!"

And so, these men of Indostan
Disputed loud and long,
Each in his own opinion
Exceeding stiff and strong,
Though each was partly in the right,
And all were in the wrong!

Saxe's poem of six blind men attempting to define what exactly is an 'elephant' reminds me very much of the scholarly debate surrounding public diplomacy and public relations. Each inquirer approaches the topic from a particular vantage point which ultimately influences each one's definition and concept. All seem correct, yet all seem to come up short.

Scholarly work in both public relations and public diplomacy only emerged since mid-century and occurred parallel to one another with little cross-over or integration. It wasn't until more recently that the fields began to bump into one another as the communication and cultural aspects of diplomacy became to the fore, particularly since 9/11. As scholars studied, similarities began to be noted, and questions arose as to the true relationship and linkages between the two fields. While scholarly study of the two fields are modern, the processes and practices of both diplomacy and public relations are embedded deep in human history. A quick view of history is helpful to re-orient, gain perspective, compare and contrast the two domains.

The field of diplomacy is ancient, arising from societies moving increasingly away from chaos and toward organization in search of ways to govern themselves. Deeply rooted in law, diplomacy emerged as a way to identify authoritative sources to resolve disputes and govern the relationships between states (Broderick, 1924).

Historically, the term 'diplomacy', in the professional sense, has implied the process of relations between nation states (Broderick, 1924). There are many views on diplomacy, but there is no over-encompassing theory or theoretical framework. Concepts and definitions of diplomacy are, therefore, contested. This, juxtaposed against globalization and increasing interconnectedness of the world, has left conceptualizations of diplomacy lacking. The more recent term 'public diplomacy' emerged in the mid-1960s when Edmund Gullion, a former diplomat and dean of the Fletcher School of Diplomacy at Tufts University in Massachusetts, attempted to distance the state-to-state communication process from the negative connotations of propaganda (Cull, 2008). In spite of the attempt to distinguish, it has always been understood that the term refers to traditional views of diplomacy of general state-to-state relations, which some also call 'classical diplomacy' or 'traditional diplomacy'. In 1980, the United States Government called "public diplomacy a new label for an old concept. . . . It supplements and reinforces traditional intergovernmental diplomacy, seeking to strengthen mutual understanding between peoples through a wide variety of international communication and educational and cultural exchange programs" (International Communication Agency, 1978, n.p.).

According to the *Oxford English Dictionary*, the word 'diplomacy' is of French origin, developed in the late 18th century and is associated with the aristocracy, or ruling classes. Dictionaries note its dual definition, one professional and one personal. It is "the *profession*, activity, or skill of managing international relations, typically by a country's representatives abroad" and/or it is "the art of *dealing with people* in a sensitive and tactful way" (Diplomacy, n.d.). It could be argued, of course, that the latter is also an element of the former.

Since the time of Gullion's proposed new nomenclature, 'public diplomacy' has begun to appear in the literature and has been the object of scholarly study, but it has continually lacked a discrete definition and having been parsed into business diplomacy, corporate diplomacy, cultural diplomacy and more; it has remained, therefore, "essentially a contested term with many labels" (Potter, 2009, p. 257; see also Saner, Yiu, & Sondergaard, 2000).

As a result, the concept of public diplomacy has 'bled into' other domains of various academic inquiry such as policy studies, mass communication, international affairs and peace studies, among others (Gilboa, 2008). One of those is public relations (for example, L'Etang, 1996). Nye's (2004) introduction of the concept of 'soft power' has particularly created porous boundaries into the field of public diplomacy. Suddenly, nation states could exert power in other ways besides by economic or military force. The insertion of soft power into the discussion of diplomacy, amidst the backdrop of an increasingly interconnected world, opened the already-tenuous definition of diplomacy to acknowledge the influences of such forces as corporatism, entrepreneurialism and culture, thereby creating many nuanced notions of diplomacy.

Scholars have been debating the convergence, similarity and/or separation between public diplomacy and public relations for many years (see Van Dyke & Verčič, 2009; L'Etang, 1996). Upon examination, the resemblances between these two fields are, indeed, striking.

Similarities between public diplomacy and public relations

Both have been identified as having roots in ancient processes which evolved into modern practice. Many examples of public diplomacy from ancient history have been identified across many cultures from ancient Egypt, Greeks, the Ottoman Empire of the 6th century, the Chinese Tang Dynasty or India of the 3rd century (see Black, 2010). Public relations in ancient history has been associated with the Rosetta Stone for touting the achievements of the pharaoh; it has been identified in ancient writings of Sumeria, Persia and Babylonia projecting prowess in battle. Some have also pointed to the persuasive efforts of early Christians as ancient public relations efforts (see Cutlip, Centre, & Broom, 2000, p. 102; Bates, 2006; Cutlip, 1994, p. xv). However, the *modern* practice of public relations or "the roots of the vocation" is traditionally identified as the around the turn of the 20th century (Cutlip, 1994, p. xvi).

L'Etang (2009) identified some broad linkages between public relations and public diplomacy—communication, stakeholder relationships and shaping of public opinion. Signitzer and Wamser (2006) pointed out the strategic communication aspects. Other discussions have suggested that both public diplomacy and public relations involve dialogic communication, relationship building and the promotion of good will to create positive environments, and both aim for similar goals (Signitzer & Coombs, 1992; Wang, 2006a; Fitzpatrick, 2007; Signitzer, 2008; L'Etang, 2009; Yun & Toth, 2009; Fitzpatrick & Vanc, 2012). Public diplomacy involves "representation, advocacy, image-building, delivering messages, interpreting, and explaining" (Potter, 2009, p. 124), all of which have been associated with the public relations function (Grunig & Hunt, 1984; Cutlip et al., 2000; Wilcox, Ault, Agee, & Cameron, 2001).

There are many other similarities. Both have themes of unsavory histories and roots of meaning. As far back as 1604, the negative view of diplomacy was characterized by English diplomat Sir Henry Wotton when he declared, "An ambassador is an honest man sent abroad to lie for the good of his country" (Eilts, 1979, p. 3). Public relations has had to deal with a negative image in popular opinion because of exaggeration, manipulation, propaganda and deceptions (see Ewen, 1996; Tye, 1998). This led to, among other things, the development of the four models of public relations practice and two-way symmetry as a preferred, or more excellent, form of practice (Grunig & Hunt, 1984; Cutlip, 1994; Moloney, 2006). Most recently, the issue of negative views of public relations has led to discussions about re-naming the field or focusing on the term 'strategic communication' or 'communication management' as a way to distance the field from its more unsavoury past and negative connotations (Bailey, 2018).

Modern public relations specialists have been encouraged to be proactive and preventative in their approaches versus reactive. Maintaining proper, ongoing communication and developing positive relationships in a proactive manner is a strategic approach to avoiding crises (Coombs, 2012). Like proactive public relations specialists, successful diplomats are those who treat "international diseases at the beginnings and at their roots" (Brown, 2011, p. 75). Successful diplomatic efforts, like good public relations efforts, are often those that will never make it into the news.

A key ingredient to success in both public relations and diplomacy has been the admonition for truth telling. Public relations practitioners are held to ethical standards that include a commitment to accuracy, as evidenced by the common themes of *accuracy* and *truth telling* present in many professional codes of conduct (Yang, Taylor, & Saffer, 2016). Truth telling has also been regarded as a central key to success in diplomacy. As early as 1823, an Envoy received exhortation that "you must at all times, and on all occasions, speak the truth, for the consequence will be, that you will never be believed" (A lesson in diplomacy, 1823, p. 224). Diplomacy is "not a science based on duplicity or cunning" any more than is public relations (The relation of diplomacy, 1902, p. 160).

One purpose of public diplomacy is to "strengthen mutual understanding"; a purpose of public relations is to work toward "mutually beneficial relationships" (International Communication Agency, 1978, n.p.; Cutlip et al., 2000, p. 6). Public diplomacy requires the "assessment of public attitudes and opinions"; similarly, symmetrical models of public relations require the gathering of outside opinion as necessary research prior to developing campaigns (International Communication Agency, 1978, n.p.; Grunig & Hunt, 1984).

Public diplomacy is ongoing and continual, seeking to inform and promote understanding; public relations, similarly, has been called the ongoing process of relationship management (International Communication Agency, 1978, p. 1; Ledingham & Bruning, 2000). Golan's (2013) integrated public diplomacy model focuses on the relational aspects of public diplomacy (versus, for example, the media aspects). Successful public diplomacy involves trust, a dimension of relationships; trust has been named as an indicator of successful public relations (Payne, 2009, p. 580; Hon & Grunig, 1999). Public diplomacy has been called a "two-way street" as has public relations (Payne, 2009, p. 582; Snow, 2005; Goldman, 1948; Grunig & Hunt, 1984). Public diplomacy has been characterized as (critically, 'too often') unidirectional; similarly, public relations has been criticized for its history of being heavily one-way and asymmetrical (Payne, 2009; Goldman, 1948; Cutlip, 1994).

Kingsley, as early as 1967, and more recently Brown (2011) have noted the effects of semantics and language in the execution of public diplomacy. Public relations scholars have embraced theories of communication such as symbolic interactionism and have recognized the process of creation of meaning and semiotics as playing a role in successful communication practice (Braun, 2012; Gordon, 1997; Anderson, n.d.).

The origins of public diplomacy are in state-to-state communication, and, it has been suggested, similarly, that public relations activity "largely originated with the state [as] the only organization with the resources and need to organize large-scale public communication to shape perception on policies, religions, and its underlying legitimacy" (Senne & Moore, 2015, p. 327).

Indeed, many of Cull's (2010) lessons for "a new public diplomacy era" (p. 11) could virtually read as lessons in public relations:

a it begins with listening
b it is connected to policy (i.e. objectives)
c it is not a performance for domestic consumption
d it requires credibility
e it is 'not always about you'
f it is everyone's business

Finally, interestingly, the public relations function has been viewed as an ambassadorial function, and empirical testing has shown linkages between public relations behaviour and management and diplomacy behaviour and management (Carmi & Levental, 2019; Yun, 2009).

In view of these many similarities and points of intersection, including others, it is predictable that linkages between public relations and public diplomacy have been the subject of scholarly inquiry (also see Bouzanis, 2009).

The key puzzle pieces: select linkages

Linkage #1 – propaganda as neutral

In spite of many scholarly efforts, what is preventing the linkage between the fields of public diplomacy and public relations? The negative image of public relations as being a credible source of information has been named as a stumbling block or barrier to the integration of the professions (Snow, 2015). The public relations profession has evolved considerably since its early days of largely one-way, asymmetrical approaches and its perception as largely manipulation and flack, but still, ironically, suffers from an image problem. This image problem lies largely with the values-laden definition of propaganda as a negative, versus neutral, term. Scholars have discussed propaganda as a neutral term, more akin to a one-sided presentation (Moloney, 2006, p. 167). Propaganda exists in government communications as much as business, or even non-profit communications. Such exhortations to 'don't text and drive', 'don't smoke' or 'please vaccinate' can be viewed as no less propagandistic than Hitler's mass deceptions of WWII; in other words, propaganda is one-way communication to achieve the sender's purpose, with asymmetry as not necessarily unethical, depending on the communication (Yun, 2009). The question of the morality of an appeal is a separate one that need not impinge upon definition. The idea of having separate terms for ethical versus non-ethical communications practice does exist, however, in some Eastern European countries. Practitioners in Russia and Bulgaria reference the existence of 'black PR' as distinct from 'public relations' when there is an element of duplicity or intention to harm (Braun, 2007, p. 211; Samuilova, 2004).

Scholars and practitioners need to settle on the term 'propaganda' as a neutral term that carries no moral declarations with it but rather is a reflection of the direction and mutuality of communication (that is, one-way asymmetrical communication). The morality and merit of a message or campaign is another matter.

This is not so far-fetched. The term 'propaganda' has historically been a fluid term. While it originated from the Latin meaning 'to propagate' and was developed in the religious context of the Catholic Church in the 1600s, it drifted into secular contexts by the 1700s and then took on negative connotations in political contexts in modern history (Diggs-Brown, 2012). It is a term that has ridden the waves of changing cultural times. In these times of global communication, multiplicity of thought, increasing fragmentation of audiences and more communication methods than ever before in the context of a marketplace of ideas, propaganda is commonplace. Advocates, activists, advertisers and even parents produce propaganda to propagate their positions, and often the merits of a message cannot be immediately determined; one person's crusade can be one person's saviour and another person's poison. A view of propaganda as a neutral term, devoid of judgement, and which simply indicates the direction and mutuality of a piece of communication, could help public relations shed its negative image. Propaganda could be more accurately viewed as a natural part of the overall communication process that actually occurs in many contexts, not only in public relations.

Linkage #2 – public relations as communication management

Definitional issues, like one's view of propaganda, have likely produced the greatest hindrance to sorting through the relationship and linkages between public relations and public diplomacy. Both fields have suffered crises of definitions. As noted by international broadcaster Kim Andrew Elliott, "The term 'public diplomacy' is now attributed to so many activities that it has lost useful meaning" (Elliott in Brown, 2011). Public relations has followed suit; it has no fewer than 500 definitions. If something can mean so many things, then it doesn't mean anything at all. Both fields have been challenged with this glaring question.

For a time, and perhaps still in the minds of many, the term 'public relations' has led people down a particular perceptual path when it attempted to move from a technical function to a managerial function. Cutlip, Center and Broom (1985), in their classical definition, called public relations "the *management* function that establishes and maintains mutually beneficial relationships between an organization and the publics on whom its success or failure depends" (p. 4). Grunig and Hunt's later (1984) definition was more parsimonious: "Public relations is the *management of communication* between an organization and its publics" (p. 6). Only recently, with public relations more finely explicated and emphasized as 'communication management' has this distinction become sharper, achieving resonance and gaining popularity (Bailey, 2018). Public relations people are indeed, 'managers', but they are managers of *communication* – not of policy, not of people, not of distribution channels, not of revenues, or any other aspect of an organization (although they can *influence* these through the process of the feedback loop as a result of listening and information-gathering and then information sharing with appropriate managers).

Communication management (aka public relations) is a process and a function that occurs in many contexts, including businesses, corporations, non-profit groups, activist organizations and governments. Public relations has often been labelled more specifically according to the specialized context in which it functions (e.g. *corporate* public relations, *non-profit* public relations, *government* public relations), but, structurally, they can all be viewed as subdivisions of specific types of communication by context that exist under the larger umbrella of the domain of public relations. Specific nomenclature has been, and should be, more of an indication of the context in which the communication functions and not a distinctive of the communication function itself. Cutlip and Centre (1971) recognized early on that public relations could be baffling to others because it was a conglomeration of many parts that could easily be confused and subsumed by its own subdivisions. "Public relations is often confused with and used as a handy synonym for some of its functional parts such as publicity, press agentry. . . . These may be parts . . . but the sum of parts does not equal the whole" (p. 3).

The field of public diplomacy could be viewed as a context in which public relations functions, much like public relations or strategic communication occurs in non-profit contexts or corporate contexts (Snow, 2015; Golan & Yang, 2015). However, if public diplomacy is viewed as a context, what is that context, and how is it defined? Perhaps by identifying what public diplomacy is *not*, we can get to a more discrete notion of what public diplomacy *is*. It is certainly *not only* about communication and relationship management because all fields require some aspect of this. The differentiators of the public diplomacy field from any other field are the policy development, foreign affairs and the national interest aspects as the particular context in which the communication functions (Snow, 2015). Public diplomacy involves the nation, the law and the development of foreign policy that govern relationships between states.

Linkage #3 – fine-tuning and re-defining public diplomacy

To extend Snow (2015), and in light of the above discussion, public diplomacy, as we have come to understand it collectively as a scholarly community, could be re-conceptualized as a broader term that encompasses two parts. It is (a) the development of foreign policy to further the national interest, that utilizes (b) the strategic management of the communication (i.e. public relations) around that foreign policy to external audiences in pursuit of the national interest. This can be supported as Broderick (1924) identified classical diplomacy as "the art of conducting international affairs between States" and is "*only one* of the instruments of statesmanship"

(Broderick, 1924, p. 68). Zaharna (2009) noted that "public diplomacy is as much a communication phenomenon as a political one" (p. 86). Statesmanship requires many instruments, including both (a) the development of excellent policy and (b) the use of effective communication around those policies. You can't have one without the other.

If such a two-pronged definition of public policy can be accepted – one that identifies its context and also acknowledges the closely intertwined and critical aspect of communication that surrounds the context – there would be no need for the more specific term 'public diplomacy'. The historical, more generic term, 'diplomacy', would suffice. Earlier definitions of diplomacy are more general and more in line with popular cognitions, anyway: Diplomacy is "the art of conducting international affairs between States" (Broderick, 1924, p. 68). The term 'public diplomacy' would not be needed as the reason for the more specific nomenclature, as described by Cull (2008), originated from issues of communication, specifically, to distance the communication process from negative views of propaganda. (Further to these discussions, if 'propaganda' were to be viewed as a value-free, neutral, term, this would further diminish the need for the term 'public diplomacy'.)

While historically diplomacy (also known as traditional diplomacy or classical diplomacy) has implied direct state-to-state relations, increasingly it has grown to involve non-state actors like businesses or non-governmental organizations (Melissen, 2005). Much debate has ensued about the role of non-state actors in achieving diplomatic outcomes. If we were to revert to original conceptualizations, diplomacy could be viewed more traditionally as direct state-to-state relations, and the term 'public diplomacy' could be re-conceptualized to encapsulate diplomatic contexts with primarily non-state actors and audiences as purported by Snow (2009) and the Centre for Strategic and International Studies (2007): "The intent of public diplomacy is to communicate with the people, not the governments, of foreign countries" (p. 47).

Linkage #4 – public diplomacy as a sub-field of international relations

The strongest placement for public diplomacy on the scholarly landscape, considering its context of cross-border relations and its heavy reliance on the communication function, lies within the subdivision of international public relations (Potter, 2009). Public diplomacy has been described by the U.S. State Department as "engaging, informing, and influencing key *international* audiences about U.S. policy" (see Brown, 2011). It has also been suggested that international public relations even becomes diplomacy "if governments either become involved actively and visibly as co-sponsors or in a more lowkey but nevertheless supportive fashion, such as when embassies provide behind-the-scenes advice on local conditions and audiences" (Potter, 2009, p. 33). And, conversely: "If a government provides general direction, resources, or strategic advice, then public relations events and programs in other countries become part of a country's public diplomacy" (Potter, 2009, p. 34).

A quick view of the most rudimentary understanding of diplomacy supports its conceptual similarity to international relations. 'Diplomacy' is classified (a) as a noun and defined as "the profession, activity, or skill of managing *international relations*, typically by a country's representatives abroad", and (b) as "the art of dealing with people in a sensitive and effective way" (Diplomacy, n.d.). When putting these two aspects together, it is a basic depiction of how many people view traditional diplomacy. The definition would also serve as an understanding of international public relations. Potter (2009) noticed this when he espoused public diplomacy as "international public relations practised by government" (p. xi).

Fitzpatrick and Vanc (2012) have suggested that the two fields of public relations and public diplomacy have divided; however, this further illustrates the heavy and ongoing cloud of murkiness that results from viewing a field from only the vantage point of its communication process. Hearkening back to our Indian parable, one man touched the elephant's side and called the elephant a 'wall'; another man touched the tusk and declared the elephant was a 'spear'. An entity cannot be defined against itself. The field of public diplomacy cannot be defined by its communication function; it must be defined by its context and the characteristics that make it is a discrete field. Rather than public relations and public diplomacy having divided, it seems more likely that public relations has always been functioning within the context of public diplomacy (as strategic communication management, if you will) but has not been recognized. Public diplomacy has failed to recognize its communication arm as public relations; additionally, public relations has failed to identify and study the function of strategic communication management within the specific context of public diplomacy. Public relations scholars have danced around it, studying non-governmental organizations, government-to-people campaign analysis, region-specific practices (see Molleda & Askin, 2005; Jain, De Moya, & Molleda, 2014) or as personality-centric with focus on such political figures as Germany's Otto von Bismarck, Canada's William Lyon Mackenzie King and the United States' Dwight Eisenhower (Senne & Moore, 2015; Hallahan, 2003; Parry, 2014). But public relations scholars have not directly recognized the diplomatic context as a specialized context by which to study the application of communication. In other words, while we have studied health communication, or government communication, or marketing communication, we have failed to recognize and name the concept of diplomatic communication.

Linkage #5 – the nation-state as an administrative organization

Aside from the many cross-associations between the fields of public diplomacy and public relations and aside from the definitional issues, to further juxtapose the two fields, it may be helpful to view the nation-state as an organization from a systems theory and organizational theory perspective. "The nation state is a system of organization in which people with a common identity live inside a country with firm borders and a single government, which as, as a part, the state (system of government) and the nation (its people)" (Muscato, 2018). A nation-state is a "territorial form of political organization" (Malešević & Pavasović Trošt, 2018).

Countries have been viewed as organizations through the lens of organizational theory. One study examined the country of Egypt from this perspective with the "vision of the nation-state as an organization and oriented toward solving the problems faced by that organization" (Heaphey, 1966). Max Weber, in his well-established sociological work, *Economy and Society* (1922), refers to a nation-state as an *organization* dealing with issues of power, violence and control within its own borders and which defends itself if attacked by other states.

The term 'organization', unfortunately, also suffers from a crisis of definition, having been viewed from various perspectives such as general business, organizational behaviour, economics, organizational psychology and organizational communication (Greenwald, 2008; Lundgren, 1974; Harbison, 1956). However, organizations usually involve (a) systems or structures; (b) people; (c) an identifiable mission and/or objectives; (d) management, or a body of officials; (e) consciously coordinated tasks *and* activities; (f) processes that involve planning, coordination and control and (g) the handling of economic uncertainty (see Greenwald, 2008, p. 6; Lundgren, 1974, p. 7; Harbison, 1956, p. 365). In terms of contextualizing the nation-state as an organization, and to apply these concepts to our discussion of a nation state as an organization: the *system* or *structure* is the government; the *people* are the diplomats and government workers; the *mission and/or objectives* are the foreign policies created by the government; the *management* system and *body of officials* include various administrators such as Secretary of State; its *tasks* and *activities* are all the identified activities arising from the execution of its policies; the execution of the tasks require *planning, coordination* and *control*; and the *economic uncertainties* of the context are the economic health and economic interests of the nation-state that arise as a result of foreign policy initiatives. Nation-states are specific, and unique, types of organizations in the same manner as corporations, non-profit groups, multi-national corporations or non-governmental organizations are specific and unique types of organizations (Potter, 2009; Golan, 2013).

All organizations engage in communication activities in support of their existence and furtherance of organizational objectives. The strategic management of these communications are their public relations and communications efforts (Cutlip et al., 2000).

It becomes clear, then, why the field of public relations seems to be consistently informing the field of public diplomacy (Wang, 2006b). It is because public relations is the critical, necessary communications arm of the field and context of diplomacy, without which, diplomatic objectives cannot be achieved. Insiders agree. Edward R. Murrow, journalist for CBS, as a director for the United States Information Agency in the Kennedy administration, said in an address to the Public Relations Society of America: "We are both in the business of persuasion" (as cited in Snow, 2015, p. 74). Public diplomacy's communication function is so intertwined with its mission as to become almost indistinguishable and sometimes even appearing as one and the same, depending on from what vantage point the field is viewed, much like Saxe's six blind men and the elephant.

The need to understand communication theories and processes in an increasingly global, multi-cultural and challenging communications environment, particularly since 9/11, that has driven us deeper into the examination of public diplomacy and public relations, giving rise to the questions we grapple with here today.

Putting it all together

Amalgamating issues of definition, associations and areas of linkages, the following conceptualization of the relationship between public diplomacy and public relations (aka strategic communication) is offered. In Figure 1, diplomacy is defined in terms of both its context critical and the critical role of the strategic communication process. Two types, or subsets of diplomacy are then highlighted (public diplomacy and traditional diplomacy) and their nuances proposed, in line with our discussion. The critical process of strategic communication (aka public relations) to effect diplomacy is illustrated as foundational and common across all types of diplomacy. There are some similarities of this proposition to Snow (2009) with some variation around the communication component. Whereas Snow (2009) associates one-way

DIPLOMACY

Definition: the development and advancement of foreign policy supported by the strategic management of the communication around foreign policy to external audiences in pursuit of the national interest

Public diplomacy	Traditional diplomacy
government-to-people; people-to-people	state-to-state
non-state actors	state actors; talks and negotiations
foreign policy support and advancement; unofficial	foreign policy development and advancement; official
soft power	hard power
serendipitous; flexible; experimental; residual/ripple effects	control; predictability
business diplomacy, cultural diplomacy, economic diplomacy, corporate diplomacy	smart power
audiences, publics, stakeholders	governments, consulars, embassies
communication	security
practitioners	diplomats, ambassadors, envoys, Secretary of State
organizations other than governments (nongovernmental organizations, multinational corporations, non-profits, enterprise, corporations, businesses, and so on)	governments as organizations

Strategic communication is foundational to diplomacy - All diplomatic efforts have a foundation of/are supported by strategic communication (persuasion, relationship management, public relations, interpersonal communication, mass communication, contingency theory, one-way, two-way, symmetrical, asymmetrical, mutual understanding, organization, international affairs, foreign affairs, advancement of national interests, etc.)

Figure 1.1 Definition and orientation of diplomacy and the role of public relations (aka strategic communication)

and asymmetrical communication models to traditional diplomacy and two-way practices of communication to public diplomacy, in the conceptualization following, the communication component, as has been argued here, is treated separately from its context, suggesting that one-way or two-way communication can occur in any type of form of diplomatic context.

The communication function in the table is depicted as isolated from the context to illustrate its support function to the context. If the goal of public diplomacy is to simply gather support for a nation's position (that is, to only gather support for one's cause), this it is more akin to one-way models of communication practice and counter to the foundational aspects of two-way symmetry that some put forward as a relational theoretical approach for public diplomacy (such as Ki, 2015). Diplomacy cannot be viewed as the communications and actions of a nation-state with the sole purpose to have other nation-states 'come their way' on issues to gain support. Let's not be fools, though. Although "full symmetry does not exist in the real world", processes of negotiation are part of the diplomatic process (Zartman, 2016, p. 207). Public diplomacy cannot be parsed to mean *only* one-way or *only* two-way approaches any more than public relations can be parsed in this way.

The bridge, or justification, from public relations theory is contingency theory (Cancel, Cameron, Sallot, & Mitrook, 1997). Public diplomacy, like public relations, or even *as* public relations, can be either one-way or two-way, symmetrical or asymmetrical (or any degree in between), *depending on the situation.* The direction or intention of the communication function that supports the context of public diplomacy cannot be a qualifier of the definition of public diplomacy or it threatens to alienate entire sets of relevant literature that fundamentally characterizes diplomacy as either one way or two way. There are many theoretical frameworks for diplomacy. Some are relational (Yun & Toth, 2009; Melissen, 2005; Ki, 2015), some are mediated (Entman, 2003), some are integrated (Golan, 2013). They can all situate themselves on the scholarly landscape with a two-part definition of diplomacy: one that acknowledges context *and* communication. A two-part definition of diplomacy, one that recognizes both (a) the context and (b) its critical communication function – that is, one that includes both mission (furtherance of the national interest) and practice (through communication) – can better accommodate and embrace the many nuances of practice as well as theoretical frameworks, disentangling the communication process from it context and providing a bit of clarity and, hopefully, agreement in already-cluttered scholarly landscape.

This conceptualization of a multi-part definition for diplomacy provides a clearer understanding of the relationship between the two domains and opens the way for more appropriate linkages to be established between public relations and public diplomacy. Through greater parsimony, a twofold definition acknowledges the complexity of the field of diplomacy as equal part foreign relations and communication. It identifies traditional diplomacy's differentiator as foreign policy development and state-to-state relations, and it juxtaposes the two disciplines of public relations and diplomacy in relation to each other, diminishing neither.

A multi-part definition is necessary in light of cognitive entanglement. It also allows for the many vantage points and entry points of scholarship into the discussion of public relations and/or diplomacy, whether it be investigation from a mediated communication, relational, government-to-government or people-to-people approach of public diplomacy (see, for example, Payne, 2009). This approach to definition acknowledges both the independence and interdependence of one field from the other; it positions the fields more as siblings, or even better, as a couple, working together equally as two parts of a whole, placing similar importance and weight on each part as equal and necessary parts of the whole, in which the whole is greater than the sum of its two parts. In other words, they can be viewed as 'the same but different', or better yet, 'two parts of a whole'.

The following case study is an example that underscores, again, the intertwining and entanglement of the two fields and why they cannot be separated and must be viewed as two distinct parts of a whole in order to be properly juxtaposed and reconciled. It is an historical case study of the Royal Bank of Canada and its public relations tool, *The Monthly Letter*, heretofore referred to as *The Letter*, which found itself as a tool of diplomacy.

2 The RBC and *The Letter*

Case history and background

Newsletters as public relations tools

Newsletters have been a popular public relations tool since around the time that the *Boston News-Letter* (often referred to as the first continuously published newspaper in British North America) was circulated in 1704, detailing news from London for American colonists. Newsletters have grown to become a public relations staple with almost every organization or industry offering one. Print newsletters evolved into e-newsletter and remain a popular public relations tool today.

Bank letters and bulletins (a type of bank newsletter) have been the traditional publications of banks to their stakeholders (including customers, businesspeople and friends of the bank) since the inception of banks. One of the oldest publications is the *Bulletin*, published by Credit Suisse of Switzerland in 1895. Early bank newsletters in the United States were published as early as 1917. Others include the National Bank of Australia since 1926, the National Bank of Egypt since 1948, the Industrial Bank of Japan since 1949 and the Banco Nacional de Mexico since 1925 (Welch, 1991).

In Canada, the Bank of Montreal, Canada's first bank founded in 1817, produced the *Business Review*. According to Michael Zimmerman, team lead, Acquisitions and Collection Management of the Scotiabank Records and Information Management Office, Scotiabank was founded in 1832 as the Bank of Nova Scotia and produced its *Monthly Review* from 1927–1982 (email communication, October 10, 2017). The Royal Bank of Canada (RBC) published *The Monthly Letter* from 1920–2008 (RBC, 2019a).

Welch's (1991) study of 60 bank letters from around the world showed that, while each bank letter was somewhat unique in its specific content and could range from four pages to 100 pages, they were marked by traditional types of content like "a narrative summary of state, regional, or national economic and financial conditions . . . government policies, inflation rates, trade balances, employment, manufacturing, and investment . . . predictions of trends in the economy including changes in interest rates, wages and prices, and government monetary policies", including commentaries (p. 7). They also included such items as international economic statistics, "balance sheets, profit and loss statements and the loans and other transactions of the issuing bank", with most focusing on their own "state, region, or country of origin", "few" that featured other countries, and "several" focusing "solely on international economic conditions and issues" (p. 8).

Bank letters were usually written by trained economists providing economic news of the day. The communication style reflected the rather staid profession (Welch, 1991). While the information communicated by bank letters was often considered 'dull', it was highly sought after by certain audiences and, therefore, they became housed by libraries, and often specially ordered by institutions. Bank letters were usually offered free of charge with some banks eventually charging a fee for them. Foreign banks sometimes provided English translations of their publication (Welch, 1991).

The RBC and *The Letter*

Among Canada's banks is the consistently iconic RBC. RBC had its beginnings in Canada in 1864 as a private entity, Merchants' Bank. It became Canada's largest bank in 1930, which it remains today, and is growing into a global brand (McDowall, 1993). It was named Canada's most valuable brand from 2014–2018 and has 81,000 employees, 16 million clients and 1,300 branches in 36 countries, ranking about 36th among world banks (Brand Finance, 2018; Accuity, 2018; RBC, 2019b).

Canada's banks are chartered banks in the sense that they all operate under the authority of The Bank Act, originally instituted in 1871, exist under certain conditions and restrictions and come under government regulation. Canada's banks are distinctive in that they must have their charters renewed every 10 years.

The beginnings of *The Letter* go to the end of WWI, when the bank established a Foreign Trade Department (FTD) under S. R. Noble. Edson Pease, then vice president and managing director of the FTD, instructed Noble to start "a monthly commercial letter reviewing trade and business conditions" (McDowall, 1993, p. 306). The 1920 genesis of the publication was described as a "business publication to convey information and commentary on financial and economic matters" with its primary audience as "the business man" (RBC, 2019a, para. 1). It was typical of other bank letters of its day but would evolve into what one scholar called an "unusual public relations effort" (Marsden, 1994, p. 41).

The publication has had some illustrious editors. Graham Ford Towers (1897–1975), a newly graduated economist from McGill University in 1919, was an early editor. Later, he would be etched in Canadian history as the first governor of the Bank of Canada, serving from its creation in 1934 until 1954 (RBC, 1994). He wrote on global economics, including the economies of Russia and the Far East (RBC, 1994). His successor, Dr. M. Marvin, also an economist, later became executive director of the United Nations Relief and Rehabilitation Administration. These editors were followed by Mildred Turnbull, of unknown background. Then F. J. Horning wrote *The Letter* until his death in 1943 (RBC, 1994). Under Horning, it managed a very respectable circulation, peaking at about 8,000 (McDowall, 1993, p. 306). It was "not, however, markedly different from other reviews issued by Canadian and British banks" (RBC, 1994, p. 2).

John Heron (December 1943–December 1975)

Public relations was serendipitously injected into *The Letter* under the editorship of John Heron. Not an economist, he had a background in journalism, writing for the *Toronto Daily Star* and *Star Weekly*. He was hired by the bank as a public relations advisor in 1940. When he was tapped to replace the deceased Horning, Heron initially declared, "I couldn't write that stuff!" (RBC, 1994, p. 2). "We more or less abandoned making the letter an economic treatise, and, instead, attempted to have it tell interestingly about features of our national life and international life" (Heron in Marsden, 1994, p. 41). Heron and his superiors turned *The Letter* into general interest essays to show that "the bank cares about other things besides money" (RBC, 1994, p. 2). *The Letter* evolved into a four-page, unsigned, general interest essay on topics selected by Heron and reviewed by management. It was devoid of illustrations and was not supported by promotion or advertising. It was distributed on bank counters, through mailing lists and word of mouth, and mailed upon written request (RBC, 1994, p. 2; McDowall, 1993, p. 306). It gradually became a global phenomenon, topping circulation at about 650,000–750,000 in the 1960s and 1970s (RBC, 1994, p. 6; Marsden, 1994, p. 44).

Heron penned treatises on a range of subjects: democracy, international trade conservation, pollution, industrialization, education, research, Canada's forests, Canadian life, agriculture, banking, retirement planning, art, positivity, youth, courtesy, dealing with criticism, family budgets, Canada's weather, good manners, home accidents, building a library and even how to write a letter. Each month's edition was a perky composition filled with unexpected delights for readers. It was peppered with quotes from philosophers, business leaders and political figures such as Edmund Burke, Sir Winston Churchill, Somerset Maugham, Queen Elizabeth I, Plutarch, John Milton, John Locke, John Stuart Mill, Walter Scott, Henry Ford,

Henry Drummond, C.S. Forester and Dale Carnegie, in a sort of exhortation meets education. What was consistent, however, was its spirited, accessible, engaging style of writing on a variety of general interest topics quite unlike the bank letters of the day. The overall success of this effort was foreshadowed by the popularity of Heron's very first edition. His inaugural December 1943 issue discussed the importance of India on the world stage. Circulation immediately spiked to 20,500 up from its usual 8,000 and prompted audience write-in compliments (Heron as cited in Marsden, 1994, p. 41). The uptick took the bank by surprise; they engaged in a subsequent test and issued three newsletters "as was sent out by other banks, and the results were illuminating" (p. 41). When circulation of the test newsletters dropped at least in half, administrators knew they had stumbled upon some type of phenomenon. *The Letter* would go on to consistent, widespread and immense popularity, being compiled into compendia, housed in libraries, undergoing translations, read by businessmen and government officials from around the world, and even re-appearing in journals (for example, *The Journal of Thermal Envelope and Building Science* reprinted some issues in 1999).

People the world over were hungery for the topics Heron chose to write about - topics that, more often than not, as Stuart's poem states, had nothing to do directly with the bank. Heron impressed and charmed audiences with his broad knowledge, quips and quotes, and his upbeat style. At his disposal, and often surrounding him in his office, was a sea of reference books. Although initially targeted to the businessman, *The Letter*'s appeal unexpectedly grew to include an array of audiences from all walks of life (including prisoners), both domestic and foreign. Heron said *The Letter* was "the most momentous thing he advised the bank to do" (RBC, 1994, p. 5). John Heron published his last issue December 1975 at the age of 79, having written 307 issues. He died in 1983 (RBC, 1994).

Following Heron's retirement in 1976, the bank struggled to find direction for the publication. For two years, they ran re-prints until they pondered the publication's fate. After weighing costs against benefits, they decided they had to continue producing it even though is cost some $300,000 per issue to produce ($1 million today, calculating for the rate of inflation) "given all the good will it created" (see Marsden, 1994, p. 44; Gray, 1994, para. 22).

Robert Stewart (January 1979–December 2003)

Heron's successor was journalist Robert Stewart, who continued his predecessor's winning formula. RBC described Stewart as "a journalist and author of wide experience who had written about everything from macro-economics to modern poetry" (RBC, 1994, p. 6). His literary range was exactly what was needed. Like Heron, he was not an economist. Stewart had served as the managing editor of *Financial Times of Canada*. He also wrote for *Dow Jones, The Wall Street Journal* and *Time*. He wrote two books – *Labrador* (1977), which was published by Time Life International, and *Sam Steele: Lion of the Frontier* (1979). He had also worked as a court reporter, theatre critic, book critic and travel writer (RBC, 1994). Stewart followed in the vein of Heron, even repeating and re-working previously covered done topics. His unique contribution to the publication was the idea to write feature profiles of famous respected Canadians. *The Letter* continued to enjoy success and was well regarded domestically and internationally under Stewart's editorship. According to RBC, "the most popular issues ever" penned by Stewart were 'The Importance of Teaching' (September/October 1989), 'Knowing How to Think' (May/June 1992), the '75th Anniversary Commemorative Issue' (January 1994), 'In Praise of Volunteers' (June 2001) and 'Mental Health Today and Tomorrow' (August 2002) (see RBC, 2019d). Stewart wrote about 136 issues.

In 1980, the bank underwent cutbacks, and it went from a monthly publication to every two months (Gray, 1994). In September 2002, RBC announced that it would move all the issues from 1943 and onwards online. They would no longer print any issues but would continue to send out any requests for hard copy back issues (RBC, 2002).

Stewart died December 28, 2003, at the age of 65; he was widely and publicly praised for his writing on the RBC publication, particularly for finding subjects that would interest readers (Gray, 1994; Hustak, 2004). The Montreal Press Club honored him by forming The Robert Stewart Essay Competition for students of journalism, communication and public relations at Canadian universities and colleges. This competition was sponsored by RBC Financial Group, the Railway Association of Canada, the *Montreal Gazette* and NATIONAL public relations (The Montreal Press Club Announces, 2006, p. 1).

The publication continued on with various anonymous authors from 2004 until its final edition, 'The Blue Planet', in February 2008. In a nod to the future, this denouement to a long and illustrious performance by a publication was an encouragement to water conservation. While no new issues are being produced, back issues remain online.

The reach and circulation of The Letter

There are no official records tracing the exact circulation and reach of *The Letter* throughout time, and some information is conflicting; however, information from various sources can be assembled to provide circulation averages and paint a bit more detailed picture as to the extent of its reach in order to establish level of influence.

In 1920, when *The Letter* was first established, it was a traditional newsletter under the direction of an economist, and with a specialized audience of business professionals, it had a peak circulation of 8,000 (Heron in Marsden, 1994, p. 41).

By 1941, F. J. Horning, Heron's predecessor, noted that coverage of *The Letter* in Canada was "coast to coast . . . in the rural press . . . in the daily press in urban centres . . . in financial and trade journals" with "'similar coverage in the US and Great Britain'" (Heron as cited in Marsden, 1994, p. 41). As Heron took the helm, his version of *The Letter* would enjoy a good base of circulation upon which to build. The December 1943 issue jumped to a circulation of 20,500. At that time, RBC had about 700 branches in 15 countries, mainly in Canada, the Caribbean, South America and Latin America. Circulation varied by issue, depending on the topic and the number of write-in requests, but by the late 1940s, it was averaging about 55,000 (Marsden, 1994). Success continued, leading RBC chairman James Muir to declare in 1948, "There is no doubt that this monthly letter has excellent public relations value" (Muir as cited in Marsden, 1994, p. 42).

In the 1950s, circulation grew to 150,000 with an RBC presence of about 79 branches in 74 countries (RBC, 1994, p. 2). The 1960s saw circulation at about 650,000–700,000 with about 100 branches, and by 1973, circulation was at 750,000 to readers in 100 countries (Marsden, 1994).

The 1980s saw cutbacks, and editions were reduced by half to six per year, slashing circulation down to 100,000. Subsequent write-in protests expanded the mailing list again, and the 1990s saw circulation at about 230,000 (197,000 of that in Canada and 33,000 overseas) and with RBC's presence of 1,600 branches worldwide in 75 countries (RBC, 1994, p. 6).

The new millennium, the 2000s, saw the RBC with an average of 1,300 branches in 36 countries; *The Letter* ceased printing in 2002, going fully online, with its final installment in February 2008.

In addition to basic circulation numbers, the reach of *The Letter* was often multiplied by the publication of compendia, re-prints, translations and audio recordings, which RBC could never effectively track. For example, the circulation of the compendium, *The Communication of Ideas*, published in 1950, added an immediate spike in circulation of 390,000 copies to *The Letter* (McDowall, 1993, p. 306).

By 1994, translations of *The Letter* included French, Japanese, Swedish, German, Spanish, Portuguese, Turkish, Hindi, Danish, Finnish, Italian, Hebrew and Dutch (RBC, 1994; McDowall, 1993, p. 306).

The Letter was also "reprinted in publications around the world, from small specialized newsletters dedicated to the raising of canaries and the study of Sherlock Holmes, to mass circulation magazines such as *Business Week* and *Reader's Digest* . . . included in a number of textbooks and in anthologies of Canadian writing", and it was even reprinted by competitors; in 1952 for example, 11,000 copies of the issue 'The Making of an Executive' were enclosed within the *Bank of Montreal Staff Magazine* (RBC, 1994, p. 2).

In 1977, the *Institute for Lederskab Og Lonsomhed* published a book of RBC's essays in Norwegian. This was followed in 1982 by another collection published by Business Education Institute Pty. Ltd. of Melbourne, Australia, titled *A Vision Splendid*. The institute's president, Roly Leopold, wrote in an afterword to the book: "These letters with their wisdom, richness and abiding values, are a real help, not only for ourselves but for our family, friends, associates and all whom we influence" (RBC, 1994, p. 6).

With its re-prints, translations and write-in requests and factoring in pass-along rates, it is impossible to measure the newsletter's exact reach, other than to say it was very popular in its time, and it was extremely popular both domestically and internationally.

Audiences of The Letter

The audiences of *The Letter* were as broad as its reach. It always strongly appealed to business men, whether domestic or foreign, with such titles as 'The Making of an Executive' (October 1951), 'Constructive Salesmanship' (July 1952), 'Business Development' (June 1954), 'Managing a Small Business' (June 1955), 'Money Management in Small Business' (September 1955), 'About Being a Leader' (October 1957), 'On Being a Junior Executive' (November 1960), 'Improving Managerial Skills' (July 1972) and 'Teamwork in Business' (January/February 1982). Such titles would be equally appealing to the newly emerging audience of business-oriented women mid-century, owing to the second wave of feminism.

But other audiences, whether domestic or foreign, could certainly find interest in other kinds of articles such as 'What is the British Empire?' (May 1944), 'What is Canada?' (December 1944), 'Youth Today' (April 1947), 'Let's Preserve Family Life' (November 1951), 'Mental Health' (March 1952), 'Growing Old Successfully' (December 1955), 'Analysing a Problem' (March 1956), 'Discipline in Life' (May 1958), 'Pollution of Water' (September 1961), 'Courtesy in Correspondence' (October 1965), 'What Do You Want out of Life?' (December 1971), 'The Need for Music' (July/August 1981), 'Knowing How to Think' (May/June 1992) and 'The Reality of Aging' (February 2006).

With each publication, audiences would express their pleasure, or displeasure, by writing in. This was the bank's way to gauge audience interest and characteristics. Heron once reported that feedback was carefully collected, compiled and analysed and that he received about 8,000 complimentary letters per year (Heron as cited in Marsden, 1994, p. 44). These letters were said to have come "from Yukon to Nigeria", from people in all walks of life including "prisons, convents, [and] aboard ships", including such readers as "U.S. congressmen and Argentinean naturalists" (RBC, 1994, p. 6; McDowall, 1993, p. 306).

The Letter was also consumed by those in power, as reported in the RBC January/February 1994 issue: When an opposition member proposed to read an excerpt from *The Letter* in Canada's House of Commons in the 1950s, he was silenced with the words: "We all read that!"(p. 2). It has also been recognized in legislative circles in the United States. In 1979, then Senator Edmund Muskie read a Royal Bank essay entitled 'God Bless Americans' (August 1979) into the U.S. Congressional Record. *The Letter* was also known to have been a common piece of literature tucked into the briefcases of diplomats and trade representatives (RBC, 1994, p. 2).

This historical review establishes the uniqueness and worldwide appeal of *The Letter* and records its somewhat serendipitous inception and its organic evolution. Heron and administrators had no idea of the journey they were about to embark upon when the publication took its essay format and came under the direction of a journalist and publicist in the person of John Heron. Later, under Robert Stewart, *The Letter* was able to maintain its popularity and retain its distinct brand. As late as 2002, RBC reported that even though issues had gone completely online, it still received requests at the rate of "about one request every day of the work week" for back issues (RBC, 2002, para. 4).

Because of its popularity, it reached far into the highest and most influential echelons of society, putting *The Letter* in a prime position of influence.

Part II

The Letter

On diplomatic mission

The Letter of the Royal
Has no self-serving theme.
But tends to prove that Canada
Is worthy of our dream.
The Letter which they send each month
Is good, and clear, and frank.
It speaks about most other things.
But not about the Bank.
            – Richardson, 1985, pp. 4–5

3 *The Letter* and public diplomacy

'India'

Publicist Heron's premiere issue of December 1943, titled 'India', drew the attention of the United Kingdom Information Service, which re-published the newsletter as a booklet, distributing it throughout the Commonwealth (comprised at the time of Australia, Canada, India, Ireland, New Zealand and South Africa) (RBC, 1994, p. 2). During the period, the United Kingdom was the centre of the world media attention with unrest in India, most specifically, with two to three million dying of famine because of large-scale exports of food by the British to support the war and to feed its own citizens. Relations between Britain and India were strained, and the eyes of the world were watching. Additionally, Mahatma Gandhi, an anti-colonial nationalist, had just instituted the anti-British Quit India movement, which would culminate in India's independence in 1947, just four years later. At the time of Heron's writing, Britain was setting up the Famine Inquiry Commission that did not even meet until the following year, in July 1944. Mitra (2012) examined the British government rhetoric around the famine of the summer of 1943 and concluded that it used "the rhetoric of numbers, statistics and survey" as a deliberate strategy that the author calls "quantification mode" that's effect was to contain the famine crisis through the process of diminishing and deflecting (p. 153). Numbers, lists and statistics, in contrast to human stories, surrounded the famine discourse. Units such as harvests, births, deaths, numbers of relief activities, revenues and even some sets of numbers that criticized other sets of numbers were used to communicate the famine. Mitra (2012) concluded that the use of numeration was used to provide distance between the audience and the event, promoting the perception of government control and having the famine event melt into the stream of innumerable other sober global events of the day (for example, the concurrent famines of North Africa or China), essentially diminishing the tragedy (p. 155). In truth, the situation was so dire that even the typically pro-British newspaper based in India, *The Statesman*, criticized the government's use of numbers and changed its coverage to show the dying masses with an editorial in August entitled 'All India Disgrace'.

Heron's 'India' was a treatise to correct what he called a "distorted" global image of India as a "a place of downtrodden humanity" (RBC, 1943, p. 1). "As a matter of fact", wrote Heron, "India has been ahead in the world in many of the basic freedoms", citing religious freedom, women's suffrage and the presence of women in government. He reminded Canadians, a primary audience of *The Letter*, that Indians had been more like a "sister nation" fighting alongside Canada in wars and engaging in trade (p. 1). He carefully reminded readers that the British population in India was minimal, did not exceed 50,000 and was less than half that of ten years prior. The British, he wrote, had given India the best system of irrigation in the world, and many desert lands were thereby productive and fertile. There was an intricate system of railways, the growth of unions and developing education. Citing a commentator in *The New York Times*, Heron even wrote, "The British record in India as a whole has been efficient, honourable and just" (p. 2).

As a public relations tool, *The Letter* was drawing in audiences and building the image of the bank. As a public diplomacy took, it was hijacked by the British government and distributed to the Commonwealth to bolster England's image. Public diplomacy is concerned with image, identity, reputation management and relationships between nation-states (Golan & Yang, 2015; Snow, 2009; Ki, 2015); public relations is concerned with image, identity, reputation and OPRs (organization-public relationships) (van Ham, 2008; Ledingham & Bruning, 2000; Cutlip et al., 2000). If nation-states can be viewed as organizations through the lens of organizational theory, the similarity of purpose in this case between public relations and public diplomacy is striking. The fact that the British government used a public relations tool created for another context and deemed it perfectly suitable for its own purpose illustrates how tightly intertwined the two disciplines can be. It was certainly in the British government's best interest to amplify the message used in Heron's December 1943 issue of *The Letter* as a tool for national image and reputation management among the Commonwealth in the face of "strong criticism from the international and Indian front" (Mitra, 2012, p. 154). (It is unclear to determine exact circulation or whether or not Heron's reported circulation of 20,500 for this issue included the Commonwealth distribution.) Thus, *The Letter*, created as a public relations tool created to build reputation and engage customers of the RBC, found itself accidentally in the position of being used as a diplomatic tool by a foreign government to support its foreign policy. This appears to have been serendipitous and have taken both Heron and RBC executives by surprise (Marsden, 1994).

Some might argue that, definitionally, public diplomacy must directly involve a government actor, with the implication that the actor is either the specific originator or the specific receiver of a piece of communication or that government actors are on both sides of the communication (Signitzer & Wamser, 2006); however, increased involvement by non-government actors has left the definition of diplomacy contested (see Snow, 2009). In many scholarly circles, public diplomacy outcomes no longer require that the target audience be government entities, nor does it require government-to government communications, and with some saying it can simply assume some *form* of government involvement, influence or support (Potter, 2009, p. 33). Interestingly, in this case, while the United Kingdom Information Service was an actor/sender of the communicator, it was not the creator/ originator. This is not a scenario that scholars could likely anticipate outside of case study. The government organization did not produce the piece, but in circulating it, clearly implied an endorsement, turning *The Letter* into a mass government-to-government and also, simultaneously, government-to-people piece of communication utilized by a government department in support of its colonial foreign policies. The intricacies of communications within the public diplomatic context are not only complex today but have likely also been in the past, defying categorization.

Case studies can present opportunities for theory building (Lowes, 2002). Current theory and definition of diplomacy do not account for the specific scenario in which a nation-state directly utilizes communications originating from non-state actors (whether complicit or not) to advance its diplomatic goals. To advance theory building, it may be helpful to view diplomatic communication on a tier-system (and borrowing from the development of agenda-setting theory) in which *first-level diplomatic communications* are those communications created and initiated by the nation-state to achieve diplomatic objectives and *second-level diplomatic communications* are communications in which the nation-state uses the communications of *other* non-state actors to achieve diplomatic objectives, whether the non-state actor is complicit or not.

The Letter as international information service

Not only did *The Letter* get disseminated by a foreign government to groups of *other* foreign countries but it was also "widely used by Canadian diplomatic missions to disseminate information about [Canada]" (RBC, 1994, p. 2). Representatives of Canada abroad found the contents of *The Letter* to be helpful sources of information to introduce or explain Canada to others.

In fact, it is the role of some foreign representatives, such as media relations officers, to provide information and explain Canada and its government versus to advocate for its government. For some, information dissemination *is* the work of diplomacy (Potter, 2009, p. 99). Four years after the United Kingdom Information Service hijacked the 'India' issue, Heron was demonstrating an awareness of the needs of diplomats when he dedicated the March 1947 issue to Canada's diplomatic work around the world in the edition 'Representatives Abroad', writing:

> They [representatives serving abroad] must know Canada, and not just its politics. They need to know about its resources and what is being done to make them available through trade; its transportation system which carries the goods to those who wish to use them; its financial system, which handles the medium of exchange; its labour force, its capability and its capacity. They need to know the views of the provinces as well as the opinion of the Dominion; the ideas of people as well as of administrators. They should be able to talk of our social services, arts and crafts.
>
> (RBC, 1947, p. 1)

In the issue, Heron revealed his understanding of the diplomatic purposes of such information and his awareness of his own position as a potential source of information for diplomats:

> Chances of misunderstandings between nations may be lessened by interchange of information about their people. Canada, in common with the other democracies, is eager to present a complete and undistorted picture of herself. It would be fatal to rely upon anything but a full and fair exposition and explanation of the policy and cultural life of the country, and if the information is to be effective for good it must be read; therefore, it must be presented interestingly, and with broad appeal. The overseas representative looks homeward for a steady supply of creative material.
>
> (p. 4)

Heron eagerly supplied such information, likely engaging in reflection on his own publication and writing style. This gravitation toward more consciously writing for diplomatic purposes was likely spurred by the circumstances surrounding the 'India' issue a few years earlier. Heron's writing shows his deep understanding of the diplomatic implications of the publication under his control, and he did not resist entering the arena of diplomatic intention.

As Heron settled into his writing routine, Canadiana became a regular feature of *The Letter*; it was brimming with information about the little-known land of Canada – its geography, climate, population, agriculture, characteristics, opportunities, standard of living, leisure, family life and so on, such that *The Letter* was later identified in scholarship as a "tool for international education" (Marsden, 1994, p. 41). Heron could be called somewhat of a visionary in propping up the diplomatic function, as the Government of Canada has never historically taken an assertive position with respect to communicating itself to foreign audiences in the sense of nation branding. In fact, it has often bemoaned its lack of clear identity on the world stage (Potter, 2009). Diplomats of the day likely found the pub-lication a convenient and natural fit to support them in their regular work as disseminators of national and cultural information, as it was reportedly "tucked into the briefcases of diplomats and trade representatives" (RBC, 1994, p. 2). A quick review of titles shows *The Letter*'s consistent relevance to diplomats across time with such titles as 'Canada's Need for Foreign Trade' (September 1944), 'Canada's Resources, Developments and Pos-sibilities' (January 1945), 'International Trade' (June, 1946), 'Railroads in Canada' (April 1954), 'Canada is a World Customer' (June 1949) and 'Transportation in Canada' (May/June 1985). Three issues were dedicated to U.S.-Canadian relations (September and October 1946; September 1958), and two issues were dedicated to Canada's role on the world stage (October 1966 and Spring 1996). A series of issues published in 1966 also highlighted the economies of the Atlantic Provinces, Ontario and Québec, portraying them as positive places in which to conduct business.

In 1947, at the time of Heron's initial essay on the work of the coun-try's diplomats, he had studied and was keenly aware of the Canadian diplomatic landscape, specifically recording that Canada had seven high commissioners, 11 ambassadors, five ministers, two heads of missions and three consuls general, itemizing a listing of seven high commissioners' offices, 11 embassies, five legations, four consulates general, a Canadian military mission in Berlin and a civilian liaison mission in Japan (RBC, 1947, p. 2).

Not only were Canadian diplomats looking to disseminate information about their Canada to build national image, part of their diplomatic func-tion would also have been to encourage foreign trade and build positive economic relationships with other nation-states. Heron, in the June 1946 edition of *The Letter*, tackled this issue, seemingly to assist diplomats in their job. He identified obstacles to Canadian trade and proposed solutions. In the case of Australia, he wrote, the obstacle is a lack of availability of Canadian or Australian dollars by which to pay for goods (p. 3). He further names a solution: the "creation of a Canadian dollar credit in Australia, out of which purchases from this country would be financed, or immediate import of required Australian products into Canada, thereby calling into being a natural fund upon which to draw for the financing of Canada's exports to Australia" (RBC, 1946, p. 3). Of Brazil, Heron wrote of a lack of will to be trading partners, citing Maurice Belanger, Commercial Secretary of Canada's Embassy, in Brazil: "The job we haven't yet done completely is to sell those markets to Canadian manufacturers. A lot of Canadian manufacturers don't believe in the markets. They don't realize the amount of business that has been done in those markets" (p. 3). In that same edition, Heron even inserts a list of business and trade associations that any of their tens of thousands of readers in countries around the world could contact for more information, including contact information for the Foreign Trade Service of the Department of Trade and Commerce, the Canadian Exporters' Association, the Canadian Manufacturers' Association, the Canadian Chamber of Commerce, the Canadian Importers and Traders Association and the Board of Trade.

Later, in the June 1949 issue, 'Canada is a World Customer', Canada is portrayed as a vital part of the world economy with a discussion of imports/exports and Canada's reliance upon them. There is reference to the Import Division of the Foreign Trade Service, Department of Trade and Commerce and the importance of its role; the role and activities of trade commissioners is discussed; there are some statistics about imports and Canadian expenditures; there is information and statistics on Canada's imports from the United States; and Heron educates readers on issues of trade – all, of course, delivered in a lively, engaging writing style.

The Letter as mouthpiece of the Canadian government

The Letter, although sometimes 'heady' with such topics as democracy, foreign trade and investment, always aimed to be upbeat and positive. Even tough subjects such as crime or the dire need for housing in post-war Canada were presented in hopeful, yet informative and non-condescending, terms. Surrounded by a library of some 7,000 books and flanked by easy access to government sources because of the close relationship between the banking industry and the Government of Canada, Heron readily provided a quick examination and interpretation of Canadian public policy through the liberal use of government documents and sources. He mostly presented government policy more as a source of information versus strong advocacy or brow-beating. It is unlikely that the brow-beating approach would have won over Canadian audiences with their cultural penchant for low-key approaches. Either domestic or foreign audiences of *The Letter* would have many opportunities to get more than a glimpse of Canada's government positions, including both at the federal and provincial levels. As a result, foreign readers would likely get an impression of Canada as an intelligent, non-confrontational, approachable country, which is a reputation it continues to enjoy today, consistently ranking among the top brands on the Anholt GfK Nation Brands Index[SM] (NBI[SM]) (Canada's global brand, 2017).

Heron showcased Canada in partnership with the Government of Canada. I could not find one issue of *The Letter* that outrightly appeared to contradict a government position. The November 1944 edition backs up Canada's post-war housing policy, with Heron citing the Deputy Minister of Finance and referencing the Committee on Housing and Community Planning as well as Wartime Housing, Ltd. Heron takes up the government's position by reiterating that it "does not accept the views of those who believe that municipalities should engage in a vast programme of state housing financed largely by Dominion Government funds" (RBC, 1944, p. 3). In three issues – 'This is Census Year' (March 1951), 'Another Census Year' (March 1961) and 'What Use is the Census?' (March 1971) – Heron combats naysayers of the government-backed public census, quoting the law, discussing the necessity of such a course of action and citing the business benefits. He details the census form, educates the reader and encourages participation, directly quoting the Dominion Statisticians and directors of the Census Division of the time. The November 1973 issue, 'Canada's Adopted Citizens', promotes the government's multi-cultural policy of 1971 and the work of Canada's Citizenship Branch and its 18 regional offices, with quotes from the Royal Commission on Bilingualism and Biculturalism. The May/ June 1984 issue, 'Punishment and Crime', combats public perception that 54% of all crimes committed in Canada involved violence, when in fact, writes Heron, only 8% did. He writes that Canada's penitentiary system was effective, assures readers that the parole system properly screens for low-risk parolees into society and praises the newly developing system of community correctional cases, noting that "governments could not be more pleased with this movement [the community correctional movement]. . . . For financial reasons alone, the federal and provincial governments are anxious to move more of the correctional system out of the prisons and into the community" (RBC, 1984, p. 4). And 'Towards Better Mental Health' (July/ August 1991) praised the work of the nationally backed Canadian Mental Health Association.

As early as 1934, prior to Heron's editorship, *The Letter* was weighing in on public policy. It commended two bills that passed before parliament in support of government actions to ease money markets and provide for public works in order to stimulate the building industry (Royal Bank Letter Commends Bills, 1934). The position taken by *The Letter* was published in *The Globe* with *The Letter* as the focus of the story, such was the popularity of the newsletter. RBC, in the form of *The Letter*, seems to have had some public relations value as early as 1934 and was apparently only too happy to throw its public relations weight behind the federal government, potentially influencing foreign audiences and also federal-to-provincial government relations within Canada.

After Heron's inaugural issue, 'India', editors and bank administrators could not have been blind to the diplomatic and nation-building potentialities of their publication. Many diplomacy-oriented themes appeared including the dissemination of national information of use to diplomats, and the backing of policies of the federal government. *The Letter* was a consistent supporter and amplifier of one-way government information (i.e. propaganda) and was a microphone for government representatives. These messages extended across Canada and beyond, to lay people, businesspeople, investors, government representatives and nation-states with the publication's cross-national and international reach. The cosy relationship enjoyed between RBC and the federal government is additionally predictable due to the already close nature of the banks and banking system to the Government of Canada in working together to regulate the country's developing economy. Historian Duncan McDowall (1993) outlines the close relationship between Canadian banks and the government; the seedbed of the modern Canadian economy was formed jointly by the Government of Canada and the banks in a symbiotic system, and banks in Canada must have their charters renewed every 10 years.

4   *The Letter* and corporate diplomacy

Soft power

It has been recognized that, in practice, in an increasingly complex, de-regulated, marketized and highly networked world, non-state actors have evolved into potential tools of diplomacy with the capacity to participate in the diplomatic process and having power through a process of 'soft power' to achieve diplomatic outcomes (Nye, 1990, 2004; Hocking, 2004). Non-state actors such as corporations, non-governmental organizations, non-profits organizations, individuals, civil institutions and state associations, among others, have been shown to effect diplomatic outcomes, thus eroding the role of the professional diplomat as the sole and primary influence of the diplomatic function (McClory, 2017; Nye, 2004; Hocking, 2004; White, 2015).

'Soft power' is a term coined by Joseph Nye (1990) as "the ability to affect others by attraction and persuasion rather than just coercion and payment"; it is sourced in such aspects as a nation's culture, political values and foreign policy having "the ability to persuade and convince through some of the values which mankind holds dear – democracy, art, culture, human rights, welfare, good governance and societal harmony . . . thereby winning the hearts and minds of people", through the process of attractiveness, and usually developing over the medium-to-long term, "even generations" (see McClory, 2017, p. 10; Nye, 1990, 2017, p. 1; Nuri, 2017, para. 2; Potter, 2009, p. 51). Diplomatic processes, therefore, are no longer the sole domain of nation-states. In the future, a measure of a nation's international weight will be its "ability to combine hard and soft power into successful strategies where they reinforce each other" to project what Nye calls "smart power" (Nye, 2011, 2017, p. 2).

The introduction of soft power to the diplomatic landscape has led to nuanced conceptions of diplomacy, including 'corporate diplomacy'.

Corporate diplomacy and *The Letter*

The concept of public diplomacy is often associated, in both mind and practice, with corporate and business interests because foreign policy often has economic implications. Even a very early reference to public diplomacy in the book *The Public Diplomacy of U.S. Abroad: The Experience of Latin America* by Kingsley (1967), while using the term 'public diplomacy' in its title, inside the book, the author uses the term 'business diplomacy'. Even the terms 'business diplomacy' and 'corporate diplomacy' are used interchangeably, further demonstrating the lack of clarity around definition (see, for example, Saner, Yiu, & Søndergaard, 2000). 'Corporate diplomacy' has been defined as "corporations as non-state actors in public diplomacy" in which business-oriented non-state actors can work with government actors in building the image and reputation of the nation-state and/or corporation abroad, whether intentionally or unintentionally (see White, 2015, pp. 306, 310).

In our case study of the RBC and hearkening to its first issue under Heron, 'India', which was distributed by the United Kingdom Information Service across the Commonwealth, not only can the case be viewed through the lens of public diplomacy as we have already studied, it an also be viewed through the lens of corporate diplomacy. A business-oriented non-state actor (RBC) worked with (albeit likely unintentionally) a government actor (the United Kingdom Information Service) to build the image and reputation of a nation-state (the United Kingdom) abroad, particularly during a period of high political tensions. The communication occurred not only in locations where RBC branches existed but, as a result of United Kingdom intervention, among the many British Commonwealth countries.

The role of business in public diplomacy has been studied and noted as extensive, even more than a basic extension of political diplomacy (Kingsley, 1967). The corporation has had monumental effects on government relations, public diplomacy, and war and peace. Latin America is a prime example of the deep ties between its economic development and foreign business, to varying effects, both positive and negative.

Interestingly, Kochhar and Molleda (2015) situate corporate diplomacy within the field of international public relations. They do this through the concepts of *staged and perceived authenticity, localization, cross-national conflict shifting, corporate social responsibility* and *multi-sector partnerships*, also discussing the abstractions of *legitimacy* and *stakeholder* as concepts in international public relations applicable to the practice of corporate diplomacy from a relational public diplomacy perspective. This further underscores the reality that the business environment is a fine-tuned web of relationships that includes state actors (Johanson & Vahlne, 2009).

RBC *and* The Letter*: corporate social responsibility as an aspect of corporate diplomacy*

Corporate social responsibility (CSR) has been a growing area within the corporate world. "CSR is the deliberate inclusion of public interest into corporate decision-making . . . the honouring of a triple bottom line: People, Planet, Profit" (Pimple, 2012, p. 761). It has been suggested that "CSR may be a part of the process of public diplomacy that contributes to the public diplomacy of nations" (White, 2015, p. 306). CSR within the context of corporate diplomacy "may be implemented by various means . . . may include intentional coordination of effort with governments . . . are a form of soft diplomacy . . . can include actions of good corporate citizenship . . . and through socially responsible actions, can regulate global issues" (White, 2015, pp. 310, 311, 312; L'Etang, 2009; Blowfield & Frynas, 2005; Dahlsrud, 2006; Scherer & Palazzo, 2007).

A specific incident from RBC history, although not directly involving *The Letter*, supports this idea. In 1960, in Castro's Cuba, RBC was one of only two banks not nationalized under the new regime, having had a presence in Cuba since the turn of the century, establishing 65 branches and becoming Cuba's largest bank and maintaining positive relations (McDowall, 1993). After 60 years on the island, it sold its assets to Castro in an amicable arrangement and was allowed to retain an office in Havana and to finance Cuban trade. Because of its favoured status, RBC was in a position to play a role in coordinating a ransom payment of $60 million in food and medicines from the United States to Cuba during the Bay of Pigs crisis since Castro refused to deal through the American government or its banks. RBC historian Duncan McDowall (1993) recounts details of RBC's role in acting as a financial intermediary involving RBC, Banco Nacional de Cuba and the American Red Cross to pay the ransom and facilitate the repatriation of hostages. RBC waived its $70,000 fee in a charitable act (p. 365). RBC, as a corporate non-state actor, engaged in socially responsible corporate behaviour, facilitating dealings between nation-states with no apparent financial gain and no publicity, to further diplomatic outcomes.

As an offshoot of the direct activities of *The Letter*, representatives of the bank itself in the course of doing business routinely met with international government and business officials, influencing relations and advancing diplomatic objectives. In 1954, for example, RBC began relations with China, later leading to the opening of an office in Beijing in 1981. In 1956, at a time when not many were travelling there, RBC Chairman James Muir visited Russia to meet with the Soviet finance minister and the head of Russia's central bank, promoting the economic potential of Canada. RBC reports: "Muir's visit predated any similar visit by a Canadian minister of external affairs and his comments helped turn Canadian opinion on the Soviet Union, contributing to the rapprochement between East and West" (RBC, 2019c). Corporate visits to foreign states can be viewed as socially responsible acts of parties wishing to act as good corporate citizens in the world, which can lead to diplomatic outcomes. Many non-state actors are fully cognizant this is to the benefit of multiple parties; smooth relations with countries not only benefit the non-state actors but also benefit others in the society.

CSR has been likened to the conscience of an organization (Davis, 2008). John Heron said he attributed the success of *The Letter* as providing "the voice of the bank's social conscience" (RBC, 1994, p. 5).

5 *The Letter* and economic diplomacy

Economics and diplomacy are closely linked. The term 'economic diplomacy' is also a contested term. Economic diplomacy is when business leaders and state actors, such as diplomats, can sometimes work together to create a favourable business climate to benefit businesses and contribute to profits across borders (see Saner & Yui, 2003; White, 2015). The goal of economic diplomacy is to create a favourable business climate for business in general versus firm specific (White, 2015). Exports, as an economic unit, have been named as an instrument of diplomacy; exports are named as one of the six dimensions by which to rank and measure international reputation by the Anholt-GfK Nation Brands Index (SM) (others are governance, immigration, investment, people and tourism) (Ipsos, 2019).

The relationships between diplomacy and economics can be seen most clearly and strongly in the origins of the field. Broderick (1924) notes the economic features of the diplomat's work because of commercial competition resulting from rapid and ongoing industrialization (p. 77). The diplomat's function is vital to tackle the international aspects of economic interests, including the gathering of commercial intelligence. Many countries have noted this relationship and set up relevant offices. Great Britain, for instance, added a unit to its foreign service around 1915 – the commercial diplomatic service under the Department of Overseas Trade, a "joint child" of the Foreign Office and Board of Trade, which worked closely with British manufacturers and traders both domestically and abroad (Broderick, 1924, p. 77). France, Italy, Brazil and the United States followed suit.

Consular services, an arm of the government, have historically been known to gather trade intelligence, act as notaries and administrate national shipping laws, most notably with regard to the protection and human rights of seamen. This focus on the welfare of seamen, including such aspects as their general treatment, or intervention in case of legal dispute and repatriation services, formed the basis of the Consular offices as we know them today with their current focus on travel-related services (Broderick, 1924). Also, historically, consuls of Greece and Egypt were needed to act as "respected authoritative sources" for trade and commercial disputes, particularly maritime disputes, even engaging the use of witnesses and issuing formal judgments (Broderick, 1924, p. 78). England's first consul served under King Richard III in 1485 at Pisa, Italy, to serve English merchants (Broderick, 1924). Since that time, the evolution of Consular and diplomatic offices has sometimes overlapped and sometimes fused, but both play a role in protecting the national interest.

The relationships between states can heavily affect the commercial interests of a nation. An early example of this from modern history is the English connection with the River Plate Republics of South America. The region of River Plate had been engaging in trade with England at the rate of about GBP $1 million per annum, at the peak of Britain's exports to the region (Whitaker and Company, 1847). It signalled the promise of local prosperity, the provision of a steady source of goods in the absence of any extensive local manufacturing or production, and the possibilities of the benefits of some European immigration. The Anglo-French intervention of 1842 enacted a series of policy changes that escalated tensions in the region. In 1847, one analyst wrote that after five years of blockade and intervention, they had "literally accomplished nothing, but the ruin of our own and every other foreign trade to that quarter, and a great sacrifice of life and property in both Republics", declaring the 1842 blockade as ruinous to all the parties of Great Britain, France and the Argentine Confederation (Whitaker and Company, p. 38). The analyst further declared that the Anglo-French intervention and the French-forced abdication of President Oribe of Uruguay was "preventing the complete pacification" of the region by interfering in their affairs, that they had "committed a great error", and it was both a "disgrace to the diplomacy and ruin of the commerce" (Whitaker and Company, 1847, pp. 38–39). As a result of political tension, economic interests suffered.

More modern examples of the links between diplomacy and economics can be seen in the consistently tense economic relationships between China and some Western countries such as Canada and the United States. In the spring of 2019, diplomatic tensions between Canada and China over the arrest of Huawei executive Meng Wangzhou resulted in a CDN $1 billion loss to the economy. Ironically, concurrently, diplomatic tensions and trade wars between China and the United States led to a 60% increase of wheat exports by Canada to China (Wingrove & Martin, 2019).

The history of both the RBC and the RBC's *Letter* are rooted in economics. The bank itself was founded as a merchants' bank on the bustling international port of Halifax, and its very livelihood was founded upon successful trade. "The early directors and shareholders of the bank . . . were practised in despatching ships southward, laden with dry and pickled fish. They returned bearing Caribbean sugar and molasses" (McDowall, 1993, p. 165). Deeply rooted in economic systems, RBC, like any other bank, was subject to the changing tides of legislation that governed such factors as interest rates, credit, mutual funds, loans and electronic banking as a part of the economic system. Additionally, Canadian banks were birthed out of the emerging economic system of a developing Canada (McDowall, 1993). Edson Pease, RBC bank employee since 1883 and a senior administrator from 1907 to 1922, was the key advocate for a central bank for Canada at the annual meeting of 1918; this institution became the Bank of Canada, Canada's central bank (McDowall, 1993).

Being part of an economic system often required being part of a political system, as RBC bank administrators experienced when they expanded into Cuba and found themselves paymaster and banker to the Liberation Army under the government of Cuban President Estrada Palma. This account generated revenues for RBC and facilitated further bank expansion in Cuba, cultivating both political and business goodwill throughout the island. The bank consciously established branches in locations that could facilitate Cuban-American trade; for example, the expansion into Santiago and Camaguey, crucial locations for Cuban sugar and cattle production (McDowall, 1993, p. 178). As a prominent bank in Cuba (some 65 branches by 1923), RBC financed much of the island's economic activity, including sugar, tobacco and iron ore, earning its revenues by the lending process and foreign exchange transactions. As Canada's foreign trade increased and the bank expanded, it became clear that greater knowledge of import and export finance was needed. In response, RBC hired an economics graduate from McGill University, Graham Towers, to head its young Foreign Trade Department. Towers wrote many of the earliest editions of the *Letter* when it was a traditional economic newsletter (McDowall, 1993, pp. 185–186).

Banks, like other business-oriented organizations, have an interest in the healthy performance of commercial and economic environments. RBC itself experienced the benefits of growth and expansion being rooted within a democratic system. Begun in 1864 as lone bank for merchants in the international port of Halifax, by 1907 it was national, with some 84 branches across the democratic country of Canada, and had begun to expand to foreign branches in Newfoundland (not yet a part of the Confederation of Canada), Cuba, the United States (New York) and Puerto Rico (McDowall, 1993). By 1925, it had a significant presence in South America, the Caribbean and Europe, as it surged in waves of assertive entrepreneurialism to "beat the competition to these outposts of development" (McDowall, 1993, p. 2).

A healthy economy is also a core concern of nation-states. These shared objectives naturally bring governments and banks and other large businesses together, including the Government of Canada and its banking system in the early days of the country's development (McDowall, 1993). Businesses require a certain environment in which to thrive. An integral part of the market-oriented capitalistic system, by its very nature, requires the proper functioning of many of the elements that can be found within market-oriented economies and which are common among free and democratic societies. Therefore, the promotion of democratic and market-oriented values in a nation contribute to the overall success of business enterprises and foster economic activity. *The Letter* consistently and enthusiastically promoted supportive themes. The issue 'Canada's Government' (RBC, 1945), written at the end of WWII, explained to readers Canada's system of democracy and promoted the democratic systems upon which much economic vitality is built, saying:

> Democracy demands more of citizens than do other forms of government. It takes for granted education, interest and high integrity. It is only in absence of these that dictators can arise, and, by holding out promises of easy and quick ways of doing things, seize power . . . acceptance of what is best in democracy, and by education in public affairs and co – operation, evolution can be continued of a system of government that will provide the race with the best kind of life and happiness.
>
> (p. 4)

'Preserving Our Freedom' (RBC, 1957) was even more direct, saying:

> Democratic freedom has failed in some countries because their people slept. It is commonplace for people who were fighting against us in recent wars to excuse themselves on two grounds: they didn't realize what was happening to their government, and there was nothing they could do but obey orders. Tyranny degrades both those who exercise it and those who allow it.
>
> (p. 1)

'Men Must Work' (January 1951) is a clear primer to readers of the basics of capitalism, the value of work, fair wages, buying power and means of production and argues with Karl Marx that the increasing mechanization of industry would *not* lower the demand for labour and would *not* result in gradual decline of real wages of the working class. 'Everyone is a Consumer' (August 1952) was schooling in the concepts of purchasing power, planning expenditures, credit, pricing, value, quality of goods, shopping, wants versus needs, wise buying and standard of living.

'Selling Your Goods and Services' (May 1965) espoused the joys of consumerism, how sales provide pay cheques, how stores distribute goods, the management and marketing process and the importance and process of market research.

'The Work Ethic is Not Dead' (September 1974) glorifies "the Puritan way of life", saying that "enlightened managers are increasingly aware of the inevitability of democracy as the pattern for a healthy society and of the importance of their role in supporting it" (RBC, 1974, pp. 1, 3).

Readers in countries such as the United States and England, who may already have held such values, would find these values being enforced, but readers in countries with non-democratic traditions or transitional governments, such as those in Central, Latin or South America at the time, where RBC had a strong presence, would be exposed to the espoused virtues of democracy and capitalism through this very upbeat, positive, non-threatening organ.

RBC and *The Letter* experienced and actively communicated capitalistic and democratic themes to foster favourable business climates for the benefit of not only RBCs growth but also the growth of other businesses.

6 *The Letter* and cultural diplomacy

As an aspect of soft power, cultural diplomacy has been defined as "the exchange of ideas, information, art, and other aspects of culture among nations and their peoples in order to foster mutual understanding" (Cummings, 2003, p. 1; Nye, 2004). Cultural diplomacy is not an entirely new concept. The term has been traced as early as 1959 to Robert Thayer, Special Assistant to the Secretary of State for the Coordination of International Educational and Cultural Relations:

> Foreign relationships are no longer relationships between government or heads of state – foreign relationships are the relationship between people of all countries – and relationships between peoples are governed by the way people think and live, and eat, and feel, and this represents the culture of a people; and so today we have in the forefront of the implementation of our foreign policy, *cultural diplomacy*, and to my mind the most important means of bringing complete mutual understanding between peoples, which in turns compels mutual understanding between governments.
>
> (Thayer as cited in Brow, 2016, para. 2)

Cultural diplomacy is "the idea is that one country becomes more favourably disposed towards another country's international policies and perspectives when it has been exposed to the country's language, culture and people" (Potter, 2009, p. 49). Culture is the face of a nation (Ralston Saul, 1994).

Cultural diplomacy is used as a means of showcasing resources, forging relationships and establishing power and position toward a political intention (Bound, Briggs, Holden, & Jones, 2007; Mitchell, 1986). It, too, however, is a contested term. It has been parsed from 'cultural relations' (Rivera, 2015). Also, there is no designated location for it within the scholarly literature a discipline.

Definitions of cultural diplomacy seem not to require the presence or involvement of state actors; the nature of cultural diplomacy is so vast, such that "governments exercise very little direct control over the total volume of international cultural exchanges" (Potter, 2009, p. 102).

Diplomacy as the transmission of culture is widely accepted, recognized and practiced. Cultural diplomacy has been parsed as a subset of public diplomacy, including government or non-government sponsored cultural activities of diplomacy (see White, 2015). Activities of cultural diplomacy are meant as a means to project, or exchange, cultural information to further diplomatic purposes. It has been viewed as a dimension, or instrument, of public diplomacy and also viewed as similar to brand diplomacy (Potter, 2009; Leonard, Stead, & Smewing, 2002).

Nations have been described as cultural systems (Iriye, 1979). Culture is one of the first aspects nations face when they encounter one another (Potter, 2009). Knowledge of another nation is achieved through media, travel, sharing lifestyle, education, tourism, study exchanges, cultural exhibits, translations and so on (see, for example, Nisbett, 2013; Mulcahy, 1999). Most often, the goal is to generate goodwill that will attract investment and contribute to economic prosperity. Part of the work of cultural diplomacy is to build a positive rapport and a foundation of trust upon which nation-states can build (Potter, 2009). Positive political outcomes are hoped-for by-products of cultural interchange.

Canada has long been engaged in the intentional crafting of its international image. Cultural messages can be an effective means of keeping a nation-state foremost in the minds of some its foreign audiences, as Canada's High Commission in London determined after a content analysis about Canada in British newspapers (Potter, 2009). During the Cold War in Canada, cultural relations was deemed so important that it replaced media relations as the primary form of public diplomacy (Potter, 2009). Canada actively promotes its culture around the world as the portfolio of the federal department of Canadian Heritage. The promotion of culture represents a "third pillar" of Canada's foreign policy behind economic growth, and international security (see Potter, 2009, p. 104). John Ralston Saul has written:

> Canada's profile abroad is, for the most part, its culture. That is our image. That is what Canada becomes in people's imaginations around the world. When the time comes for non-Canadians to buy, to negotiate, to travel, Canada's chance or the attitude towards Canada will already have been determined to a surprising extent by the projection of our culture abroad.
>
> (Ralston Saul, 1994, pp. 2–3)

Perhaps *The Letter*'s most vital role was as cultural diplomat. The publication regularly covered Canadian culture. Canadiana was one of his Heron's favourite subjects with Stewart following in his path (Marsden, 1994, p. 42). One or two issues per year were dedicated to articles about Canadian culture, geography or history with such topics as Canada's Northlands, Native Peoples, wildlife, agriculture, family life, recreation, the system of taxation, housing, youth, education, Canadian women, art, music and volunteerism. The six most popular issues of *The Letter*, as named by RBC (2019d), transmitted aspects of Canadian culture, celebrating volunteerism (June 2001), the value of civility in a culture (May/June, 1995), the importance of mental health (August 2002), critical thinking (May/June 1992), retirement (September 1978) and the 75th Anniversary commemorative edition (January 1994).

Such instructional topics supported the publication's purpose "to facilitate living in Canadian society" and "to be of service" beyond delivering economic information to readers, thereby being called "a tool of international education" (RBC, 1994, p. 1; Marsden, 1994, p. 1). International education has been identified as "a part of cultural diplomacy" (Potter, 2009, p. 98).

Successful cultural diplomacy is composed of more than just country recognition; mental constructions must elicit a response of attractiveness, whether it is as a result of a nation's economic position, immigration policies, government and so on (Potter, 2009; Nye, 2004; see Ipsos, 2019). Universal values can also serve as points of attraction. "When a country's culture promotes universal values that other nations can readily identify with, it makes them naturally attractive to others" (McClory & Harvey, 2016, p. 315; Nye, 2004). *The Letter* projected many universal values, including the value of hard work (January 1957), liberties (August 1949), avoidance of prejudice and discrimination (January 1952), the search for happiness (May 1954), the positive effects of ambition (April 1962), honesty (May 1972), the benefits of laughter (February 1979) and a discussion of morality (January/February 1984).

Part of *The Letter*'s cultural appeal was also in the agenda-setting function of its social commentary. It regularly highlighted issues of the day, including recovering from war (January 1949), world peace and the United Nations (April 1950) and the role of women in society (March/April 1992).

Canadian culture was also transmitted through the very tone of *The Letter*. Deemed by audiences to be "broad-minded, reasonable, moderate, and unpretentious", editor Stewart once responded, "Canadians are noted for seeing the other fellow's point of view, and for avoiding extremes and 'hype'" (RBC, 1994, p. 5).

The Letter: translations and exhibits

Translations are important vehicles for the export of Canadian culture (Potter, 2009; Ralston Saul, 1994). When Heron's lively pieces began to be published, they were first available in both French and English, then occasionally translated into Portuguese and Spanish and then graduated to other languages. Scholars acknowledge that while "there is little control over how translations are consumed and interpreted by foreign audiences, this lack of control legitimizes the success and quality (and hence the global diffusion) of these Canadian narratives" (Potter, 2009, p. 114; von Flotow, 2007). *The Letter* ultimately enjoyed translation into about 12 languages as it journeyed across the globe. RBC executives were particularly "gratified" and flattered when, in 1979, a Venezuelan newspaper ran an entire issue of *The Letter* about Canadian history, without attribution (RBC, 1994, p. 2).

Another tool of cultural diplomacy is exhibits (Potter, 2009). Nowhere in Canada's history has cultural diplomacy been so widespread, so significant and so apparent as the 1967 International and Universal Exposition, commonly known as Expo '67. This World's Fair was held in Montréal, Québec, from April 27 to October 20. It was Canada's debut year on the world stage and considered one of the most successful world's fairs of the 20th century for its number of attendees and nations participating (62) (Hawthorn, 2017). It was the focal point of Canada's celebration that year of its centennial, commemorating is confederation in 1867. The fervour was so intense that this event is etched into the Canadian collective consciousness. Hawthorn (2017) captures this brilliantly with the title of his book, *The Year Canadians Lost Their Minds and Found Their Country: The Centennial of 1967*. RBC was there.

As the droves of visitors came to Montréal to attend the event and to see the sites, many would have encountered the very prominent building Place Ville Marie, the headquarters of RBC, with *RBC Expo Centre* planted in the foyer. Visitors were greeted by attendants who liberally passed out maps, bank literature and city and Expo '67 information (McDowall, 1993, p. 358). While there is no historical reference explicitly naming *The Letter* as among the pieces of bank literature, given that the publication was at the peak of its popularity in the late 1960s and that it was among the bank's most requested pieces of information, boasting a worldwide circulation of about 700,000–750,000, it is difficult to imagine that *The Letter* was not among these handouts. RBC and/or *The Letter* was certainly among the swirling milieu of cultural exchanges that occurred during Expo '67, and they served as channels of cultural transmission, developing relationships between travellers, enhancing Canada's image at home and abroad and creating a sense of pride in Canadians as they constructed their national identities. Worldwide news coverage of the event would also have contributed to cultural exchange through mass media. L'Etang (2009) notes that public relations can be seen in the context of public diplomacy as a showcase of culture. Canada's Expo '67 has been regarded as one of the most notable and successful cultural exhibits in history (Hawthorn, 2017).

Connecting cultural diplomacy to foreign policy

Soft power methods, such as cultural diplomacy, can influence or impact foreign policy. John Ralston Saul, a Canadian philosopher, noted this relationship when he said, "To the extent that foreign policy is dependent on foreign public recognition – an identifiable image and a sense at all levels of what we stand for, what kind of society we are, what we sell – that policy is dependent on our projection of our culture" (Ralston Saul as cited in Potter, 2009, p. 34).

Culture has had its roots in Canada's foreign policy since 1951 with the Royal Commission on National Development in the Arts, Letters and Sciences of 1951, followed by the work of the Canadian Commission for UNESCO, then the International Service of the Canadian Broadcasting Corporation, followed by intentional cultural relations with France in the 1960s and culminating with the 1970 Foreign Policy for Canadians, which acknowledged the role of cultural activities as part of foreign policy (with focus on France, French-speaking countries and Europe) (Maxwell, 2007). Thus, by 1994, cultural diplomacy would become the "third pillar" of Canadian international relations (Potter, 2009, pp. 88, 104).

The Letter was a consistent purveyor Canadian culture from 1943 onwards; it was being disseminated around the world at the same time as Canada, as a nation, was slowly developing its cultural agenda and image abroad. *The Letter* grew alongside the development of culture as foreign policy in Canada and played its role, communicating the culture of Canada to foreign audiences through its mass mailings, translations and re-prints and distribution by its diplomats and representative abroad.

A considerable amount of cultural fare was offered by *The Letter:* 'What is This Canada? Characteristics and Opportunities' (Dec. 1944), 'Food and the Canadian Diet' (April 1945), 'Canada's Government' (June 1945), 'Canadian Women' (July 1946), 'The Canadian Indians' (July 1947), 'The Family and Its Problems' (December 1948), 'Our Canadian Way of Life' (September 1950), 'The Canadian People' (June 1963), 'Space for Leisure" (June 1967), 'The Spirit of Christmas' (November/December 1994), 'Respect for the Law" (March 1969), 'Courtesy: A Saving Grace' (September 1972), 'Canada's Cultural Riches' (June 1971), 'The Work Ethic is Not

Dead' (September 1974) and 'Canada in the World' (Spring 1996) all provided more than casual glimpses into Canada and the Canadian way of life.

An unavoidable consequence of such cultural information dissemination is the entrenchment of Canadian stereotypes. All countries must grapple with the issue of simplistic representations and stereotypes (Potter, 2009). Canada has not consistently enjoyed an extremely high profile on the world stage and has struggled with its share of myopic views (Potter, 2009). It has consistently struggled, for example, with a perception as being mainly a resource-based economy (Potter, 2009). Issues of *The Letter* such as 'Canada's Forests' (March 1944), 'Canada's Northland' (August 1944), 'Canada's Natural Resources' (June 1948), 'Our Mineral Resources' (June 1953) and 'The Canadian Shield' (November/December 1981) would entrench these perceptions. Over time, Canada has been reduced to its own unique set of symbols and stereotypical characterizations such as 'polite', 'hockey', 'maple syrup', 'sorry', 'Mounties', 'peaceful', 'cold' or 'maple leaf', Canada's national symbol (Dubé, 2017). Such abstractions were not likely helped with issues of *The Letter* such as 'Corporate Images and Emblems' (January 1962) or 'Canada and The Mounties' (Spring 1998).

While stereotypes may be mental shortcuts, they are not necessarily counter-productive to diplomacy. Through the course of time, enduring national images can support cultural diplomacy if these images are ultimately attractive. The Mountie of Canada, for example, has a symbolic association with safety and security. Images of Canada as abundant in rich natural resources have been used to entice settlers and for nation building (Francis, 2011). Depending on the semiotic associations, the value of positive enduring images can contribute greatly to a nation-state's soft power assets (McClory, 2017).

Characteristics of soft power can also include good storytelling. Identifying a national story – and telling that story well – can add to a nation's soft power (Fletcher, 2017). The best stories are those that are "aspirational and inclusive" (p. 116). Storytelling is more than just "pumping out messages", but rather it is engagement that builds trust (p. 116). Certainly, output does not equate with influence (Nye, 2004; McClory, 2017). *The Letter* has told Canada's national story from its inception in 1920 to its final issue in 2008. Each month provided a reflection and snapshot in time, revealing a piece of Canada's collective conscience. The January 1949 issue contrasted the world's scientific advancements in the face of ongoing national boundary struggles and inability of people around the world to live together peacefully. The weariness of war was reflected in the hopeful dictum of the United Nations in the April 1950 issue: "We, the peoples of the United Nations, are determined to save succeeding generations from the scourge of war". The April 1969 issue captured the essence of the decade as it explored the growing 'generation gap'. The March 1971 issue gave voice to Canadians' puzzlement with regard to the federal census. Growing affluence in the nation gave rise to discussions about estate planning (October 1971), retirement (September 1978 was one of its most popular issues), the role and value of insurance (April 1972) and how to be a lifelong learner (December 1974). The decadent 1980s were reflected in writings about business, career, selling, marketing, achievement, success and the coming 'chip technology'. The 1990s were tempered with issues on civility and knowing how to think, representing two of the publication's most popular issues. In some ways, the publication was ahead of its time, as the August 2002 issue addressed the importance of mental health; the Canadian Mental Health Commission did not make this a high priority until it unveiled its mental health strategy for Canada in 2012. Both Heron and Stewart seemed to have a fairly good pulse on the consciences of the nation and the world and, remarkably, enjoyed consistently good reception, by all accounts.

Not only content, but also delivery, has contributed to the telling of Canada's story through *The Letter*. The organ has been called an example of "extraordinarily clear and effective writing style" and has been consistently praised, over time, for writing excellence (Marsden, 1994, p. 41; The Montreal Press Club announces, 2006). For *The Letter* to effectively communicate meaningful prose, it required good writers – those from writing backgrounds such as journalism and public relations versus those from economics backgrounds – people of the pen, who could write broadly, with thoughtful consideration and elegant execution. Stewart said each four-page edition of 3,000 words took him about three weeks to write, and he called writing for the publication "the most difficult thing I have ever done" (Stewart in Gray, 1994, para. 28). Tremendous effort and skill were put into the weekly tomes, unsupported by advertising or promotion. The weight of the publication laid in its substantive writing.

The Letter as cultural diplomat was likely its greatest role as it regularly promoted Canadian language, culture, government, lifestyle, values and beliefs. Also, the sweeping definition of cultural diplomacy opens opportunities for broad analysis and interpretation of how cultural diplomacy is enacted. Even though the presence of a political actor is not required in the definition of public diplomacy, it can still be encapsulated in it: The role of Canada's Governor General in visits abroad is "an effective way of explaining Canada broad" and has been viewed as a process of cultural diplomacy (Potter, 2009, p. 108), further underscoring how definition impacts interpretation and how intertwined the diplomatic and communications aspects of public diplomacy are, as two equal and necessary parts of a whole.

7   Conclusion

Unravelling public diplomacy to see public relations

Summary

The RBC *Letter* was originally an economic newsletter that grew into a public relations tool for the bank in December 1943 when it came under the editorship of John Heron, a journalist and publicist. It became immediately popular, finding itself, even with its first issue, an accidental tool of diplomacy when the United Kingdom Information Service re-printed the issue and circulated it throughout the British Commonwealth during a time of heightened tensions with India. It became a very popular publication around the world with little promotion or advertising, growing organically through the worldwide reach of the expansion of international bank branches, word of mouth, write-in requests and through pass-along value. *The Letter* enjoyed mass appeal owing to its extremely broad range of topics, promotion of universal values, ability to resonant with audiences and its intelligent, yet lively, style of writing. Some universal values communicated by *The Letter* were around the topics of freedom, civility, ethics, honour, recreation, enthusiasm, friendship, leadership, music, service, community, honesty, courage, human relations, family life, business success and stress; they were topics that precluded gender, racial or political boundaries and were applicable to almost every strata of society.

The Letter was a ready source of information about Canada, Canadians and the Canadian way of life, serving as a convenient tool for diplomats in their regular duties disseminating information about the country, courting international trade and investment and encouraging cultural relations. Thus, *The Letter* served as a tool of diplomacy, both indirectly and directly, in state-to-state communication, state-to-people communication, and through corporate, economic and cultural diplomatic processes.

Findings and implications

While the scholarly landscape of the literature of public relations and public diplomacy may appear scattered, like Saxe's blind men attempting to seize upon the notion of 'elephant', it represents many views from specific touchpoints, which ultimately affects interpretation. The case of RBC's *Letter* illustrates the interconnectedness the field of diplomacy and its communication function.

Public diplomacy relies very heavily on its communication arm – so much so, in fact, that the two aspects have become ravelled together and fused in meaning. Zaharna (2009) noted that "public diplomacy is as much a communication phenomenon as a political one" (p. 86). A two-part definition for diplomacy would acknowledge the two equal, interdependent parts of diplomacy as (a) the development and advancement of foreign policy and (b) the strategic communication management around the context. Both are needed to properly conceptualize public diplomacy and to situate it within the scholarly landscape.

A two-part definition of diplomacy that acknowledges its unique functions (with 'policy development' at the core) and also acknowledges the criticality of the communication process, can help to unravel the communication function from the context to more clearly view the relationship and juxtaposition of one fi eld to the other.

If a two-part definition is accepted, there would be no need for the more specific term 'public diplomacy'; the general term 'diplomacy' would suffice (since the reason for the more specific nomenclature was simply to distance the field from negative views of propaganda; however, if a more realistic and neutral view of 'propaganda' could adopted, this would additionally resolve the need for the use of the term 'public diplomacy'). The term 'public diplomacy' could serve better if used to include those diplomatic efforts that involve non-state actors, as proposed by Snow (2009, p. 8). The more general term 'diplomacy' could then return to its traditional meaning of direct state-to-state communications.

A multi-part definition could unify streams of thought in public diplomacy that view the field as mediated, relational or any other. It would also resolve the literature of whether public diplomacy is inherently one- or two-way communication. Public diplomacy cannot be simply one or the other. The question of one- or two-way lies in the communication arm (i.e. public relations) of the definition, not the context arm. Contingency theory from public relations tells us that the direction and accommodation of communication of organizations 'depends' on the communication situation. Public diplomacy, like any other field, cannot be parsed to mean its communication function. Whether a nation's communication purpose is more one-way, symmetrical and propagandistic or two-way, negotiable and fluid, both options are available strategies for the contexts of either traditional diplomacy (if connoted as state-to-state communication) or public diplomacy (if connoted as communications that advance foreign policy, but do not necessarily have direct state-to-state communication). Nye (2017) reiterates that there is no superiority to either 'hard power' or 'soft power'. It is "not necessarily better to twist minds than twist arms", and "even bad people (like Osama bin Laden)" can avail themselves of the use of soft power as a choice of strategy (Nye, 2017, p. 2). It is a matter of strategy.

To conceptualize diplomacy, then, it is the development and advancement of foreign policy and the strategic management of the communication around foreign policy to external audiences (in which *classical diplomacy* is the specific context involving state actors and *public diplomacy* is the context involving non-state actors and other publics) in pursuit of the national interest.

Diplomacy could also be expressed as a specialized form of communication that operates in the domain of international publics. Other specialized forms of communication are *health* communication, *corporate* communication, *mass* communication or *marketing* communication. In the same manner that *health* communication is communication that occurs in the health-care setting or context, communication that occurs in diplomatic contexts (of either classical diplomacy or public diplomacy) – that is, for the development or advancement of national interest/national security – is *diplomatic communication*. Diplomatic communication is a form of political communication within the domain of international public relations that involves either non-state actors or nation-state actors as special publics, directly or indirectly, intentionally or unintentionally, complicit or non-complicit, communicating across borders, to achieve diplomatic purposes or facilitate diplomatic outcomes as a specialized form of public relations practice.

There is one specific potential theoretical implication from this study, for example, when actors use the communications tools of other actors to achieve their own diplomatic ends. Heretofore, diplomacy has assumed that the communications originate with the nation-state. There is no definition for a situation when the communication is essentially hijacked to achieve another's diplomatic objectives. The use of the terms *first-level diplomacy* to represent the former and *second-level diplomacy* to represent the latter may be helpful and may suggest a line of research.

The state as organization

While many linkages have been established between public diplomacy and public relations (such as relationship, direction of communication, stakeholder and so on), many of these linkages are around communication, but how can linkages be advanced by linking the communication arm of a field to the field of communication (i.e. comparing something with itself)? If the fields are to truly merge more solidly, the linkage needs to be firmly established within the arena of its distinction. Linkages must focus less on the communication aspect (part b of the proposed definition) and more on public diplomacy's reason for being (part a of the proposed definition). The concept of 'organization' can do that. If nation-states could be viewed from an organizational theory perspective with policies, mission, managers, workers and so on, it would facilitate comprehensible connection to the business literature and, in turn, situate public relations and communications as a necessary, supportive function to organizations.

The two fields of public relations and public diplomacy are too closely intertwined to be viewed simply as "cousins" (see Snow, 2009). Cousins imply distance, with loose connection and a certain level of independence. Yet they are not the same, and they are, additionally, not identical, like twins. Public diplomacy and public relations are more akin to a well-functioning couple on a mission. They are more like a team made up of two quite distinct parts working well together, so as to be almost indistinguishable. Each contributes to the whole in unique ways, and the sum of the parts is greater than its individual elements. Neither is superior to the other; each is necessary and each contributes differently. By working together, they accomplish a goal that is greater than each individual part. In true symbiotic form, there is a close relationship in which at least one party benefits; namely, the diplomatic context. Positive diplomatic outcomes are a result of the combination of good policy and excellent communication, with each informing the other. The Shared Values Initiative enacted by the United States in the aftermath of 9/11, created by a Madison Avenue advertising executive, is a case in point. While the concept was admirable (promoting to select Muslim foreign audiences the belief that Muslims were treated well in the United States as a re-branding effort to help improve the image of the United States in the Muslim world), the communication effort was ultimately deemed a failure because of unreceptive audiences and American foreign policy regarding invasions in Afghanistan and Iraq (Rampton, 2007). Diplomacy that allows the communication function to inform it leads to better policy formation and diplomatic outcomes. Such a view of diplomacy as two-pronged, in which the two prongs are of equal importance and work toward a common goal, also opens the way to examine how theoretical models of public diplomacy can draw from, and can benefit from, other theories of communication, such as mass communication theories (Golan, 2015, p. 419) or other public relations theories such as Cancel et al.'s (1997) contingency theory or Grunig's (1997) situational theory of publics.

Lastly, one of the purposes of case studies is the opportunity for theory building (Lowes, 2002). Current theory and definition of diplomacy does not account for the specific scenario in which a nation-state directly utilizes communications originating from non-state actors (whether complicit or not) to advance its diplomatic goals. To advance theory building, it may be helpful to view diplomatic communication on a tier system (and borrowing from the development of agenda-setting theory) in which *first-level diplomatic communications* are communications created and initiated by the nation-state to achieve diplomatic objectives, and *second-level diplomatic communications* are communications in which the nation-state uses the communications of *other* non-state actors to achieve diplomatic objectives, whether the non-state actor is complicit or not.

References

Accuity. (2018, May 15). *Bank ratings: Top banks in the world*. Retrieved from https://accuity.com/resources/bank-rankings/

Anderson, W. (n.d.). How to keep Rosie the riveter from contracting VD: A case study of how U.S. social reformers used public relations during World War II. *Public Relations Review*. doi:10.1016/j.pubrev.2019.05.008

Bailey, R. (2018, February 15). *Public relations as communication management*. Retrieved from https://pracademy.co.uk/insights/public-relations-as-communication-management/

Bates, D. (2006). *Mini-me history: Public relations from the dawn of civilization*. Retrieved from www.instituteforpr.org/wp-content/uploads/MiniMe_HistoryOfPR.pdf

Black, J. (2010). *A history of diplomacy*. Chicago, IL: University of Chicago Press.

Blowfield, M., & Frynas, J. G. (2005). Setting new agendas: Critical perspectives on corporate social responsibility in the developing world. *International Affairs, 81*(3), 499–513. doi:10.1111/j.1468-2346.2005.00465.x

Bound, K., Briggs, R., Holden, J., & Jones, S. (2007). *Cultural diplomacy*. London: Demos. Retrieved from www.demos.co.uk/files/Cultural_diplomacy_-_web.pdf

Bouzanis, J. (2009). *Québec's public diplomacy: A study on the conceptual convergence of public diplomacy and public relations* (Unpublished doctoral dissertation), University of Ottawa, Canada. ProQuest Dissertations. Retrieved from https://ruor.uottawa.ca/bitstream/10393/28121/1/MR52344.PDF

Brand Finance. (2018, May 24). *RBC is Canada's most valuable brand*. [Press Release]. Retrieved from http://brandfinance.com/news/press-releases/rbc-is-canadas-most-valuable-brand/

Braun, S. (2007). The effects of the political environment on public relations in Bulgaria. *Journal of Public Relations Research, 19*(3), 199–228. doi:10.1080/10627260701331747

Braun, S. (2012). Can we all agree? Building the case of symbolic interactionism as the theoretical origin for public relations. *Journal of Professional Communication, 4*(1), 49–70. doi:10.15173/jpc.v4i1.2614

Broderick, J. (1924). Diplomacy. *The Catholic Historical Review, 10*(1), 68–84. Retrieved from www.jstor.org/stable/25012044

Brown, J. H. (2011, April 24). *Public diplomacy as a linguistic phenomenon.* Retrieved from www.huffpost.com/entry/public-diplomacy-as-a-lin_b_852828

Brown, J. H. (2016). *What we talk about when we talk about cultural diplomacy: A complex non-desultory non-philippic.* Retrieved from http://americandiplomacy. web.unc.edu/2016/03/what-we-talk-about-when-we-talk-about-cultural-diplo macy-a-complex-non-desultory-non-philippic/

Canada's global brand ranks 4th in study of 50 nations: Ties with Japan. Retrieved from www.businesswire.com/news/home/20171116005474/en/Canada%E2%80% s-Global-Brand-Ranks-Fourth-Study-50

Cancel, A., Cameron, G., Sallot, L., & Mitrook, M. (1997). It depends: A contingency theory of accommodation in public relations. *Journal of Public Relations Research, 9*(1), 31–63. doi:10.1207/s1532754xjprr0901_02

Carmi, U., & Levental, O. (2019). Ambassadors in track suits: The public relations function of Israeli delegations to the Olympic games during the State's first decade. *Sport History Review, 50*(1), 17–37. doi:10.1123/shr.2018-0042

Center for Strategic and International Studies. (2007). *CSIS commission on smart power.* Washington, DC: The CSIS Press. Retrieved from https://csis-prod. s3.amazonaws.com/s3fs-public/legacy_files/files/media/csis/pubs/071106_ csissmartpowerreport.pdf

Coombs, W. T. (2012). *Ongoing crisis communication: Planning, managing and responding.* Los Angeles, CA: Sage.

Cull, N. J. (2008). Public diplomacy: The evolution of a phrase. In N. Snow & P. M. Taylor (Eds.), *The handbook of public diplomacy* (pp. 19–24). London: Routledge.

Cull, N. J. (2010). Public diplomacy: Seven lessons for its future from its past. *Place Branding and Public Diplomacy, 6*(1), 11–17. doi:10.1057/pb.2010.4

Cummings, M. (2003). *Cultural diplomacy and the United States government: A survey.* Retrieved from www.americansforthearts.org/sites/default/files/ MCCpaper.pdf

Cutlip, S. M. (1994). *The unseen power: Public relations, a history.* Hillsdale, NJ: Lawrence Erlbaum Associates, Inc.

Cutlip, S. M., & Centre, A. H. (1971). *Effective public relations.* Englewood Cliffs, NJ: Prentice Hall.

Cutlip, S. M., Center, A. H., & Broom, G. M. (1985). *Effective public relations* (6th ed.). Englewood Cliffs, NJ: Prentice Hall.

Cutlip, S. M., Centre, A. H., & Broom, G. M. (2000). *Effective public relations* (8th ed.). Upper Saddle River, NJ: Prentice Hall.

Dahlsrud, A. (2006). How corporate social responsibility is defined: An analysis of 37 definitions. *Corporate Social Responsibility and Environmental Management, 15*(1), 1–13. doi:10.1002/csr.132

Davis, B. (2008). The new corporate conscience: Corporate social responsibility. *In the Black, 78*(11), 44–47.

Diggs-Brown, B. (2012). *Public relations: An audience-focused approach.* Boston, MA: Cengage.

Diplomacy. (n.d.). *In Lexico powered by Oxford*. Retrieved from www.lexico.com/en/definition/diplomacy

Dubé, D. (2017, June 28). *Global news*. Retrieved from https://globalnews.ca/news/3550982/canada-150-6-canadian-stereotypes-that-happen-to-be-true/

Eilts, H. F. (1979). Diplomacy: Contemporary practice. In E. Plischke (Ed.), *Modern diplomacy: The art and the artisans* (pp. 3–18). Washington, DC: The American Enterprise Institute for Public Policy Research.

Entman, R. M. (2003). Cascading activation: Contesting the White House's frame after 9/11. *Political Communication, 20*, 425–432.

Ewen, S. (1996). *PR! The social history of spin*. New York, NY: Basic Books.

Fitzpatrick, K. (2007). Advancing the new public diplomacy: A public relations perspective. *The Hague Journal of Diplomacy, 2*(3), 187–211. doi:10.1163/187119007X240497

Fitzpatrick, K., & Vanc, A. (2012, August 9–12). *Public relations and public diplomacy: A divided past, a shared future*. Paper presented to the Association for Education in Journalism and Mass Communication, Chicago, IL.

Fletcher, T. (2017). *How to become a soft power superpower* [Contributing Essay]. Retrieved from https://softpower30.com/wp-content/uploads/2017/07/The-Soft-Power-30-Report-2017-Web-1.pdf

Flyvbjerg, B. (2006). Five misunderstandings about case study research. *Qualitative Inquiry, 12*(2), 219–245. doi:10.1177/1077800405284363

Francis, D. (2011). *Selling Canada: Three propaganda campaigns that shaped the nation*. Vancouver, Canada: Stanton, Atkins & Dosil Publishers.

Gilboa, E. (2008). Searching for a theory of public diplomacy. *The Annals of the American Academy of Political and Social Science, 616*(1), 55–77 doi.org/10.1177/0002716207312142

Golan, G. J. (2013). An integrated approach to public diplomacy. *American Behavioral Scientist, 57*(9), 1251–1255.

Golan, G. J., & Yang, S. (2015). Introduction: The integrated public diplomacy perspective. In G. J. Golan, S. Yang, & D. F. Kinsey (Eds.), *International public relations and public diplomacy* (pp. 1–12). New York, NY: Peter Lang.

Goldman, E. (1948). *Two-way street: The emergence of the public relations counsel*. Boston, MA: Bellman.

Gordon, J. C. (1997). Interpreting definitions of public relations: Self-assessment and a symbolic interactionism-based alternative. *Public Relations Review, 23*(1), 57–66.

Gray, A. (1994, July 18). Food for thought: Royal Bank Letter celebrates 75 years of discussing everything except banking and economics. *The Gazette*, Section F3. ProQuest.

Greenwald, H. P. (2008). *Organizations: Management without control*. Los Angeles, CA: Sage.

Grunig, J. E. (1997). A situational theory of publics: Conceptual history, recent challenges and new research. In D. Moss, T. MacManus, & D. Verčič (Eds.), *Public relations research: An international perspective* (pp. 3–46). London, International Thompson Business Press.

Grunig, J., & Hunt, T. (1984). *Managing public relations*. New York, NY: Hunt, Rinehart & Winston.

Hallahan, K. (2003). W. L. Mackenzie King: Rockefeller's 'other' public relations counselor in Colorado. *Public Relations Review*, *29*(4), 401–414. doi:10.1016/j. pubrev.2003.08.003

Harbison, F. (1956). Entrepreneurial organization as a factor in economic development. *The Quarterly Journal of Economics*, *70*(3), 364–379. doi:10.2307/1884230

Hawthorn, T. (2017). *The year Canadians lost their minds and found their country: The centennial of 1967*. Madeira Park, Canada: Douglas and McIntyre Ltd.

Heaphey, J. (1966). The organization of Egypt: Inadequacies of a non-political model for nation-building. *World Politics*, *18*(2), 177–193. doi:10.2307/2009695

Hocking, B. (2004). Privatizing diplomacy? *International Studies Perspectives*, *5*(2), 147–152. doi:10.1111/j.1528-3577.2004.00164.x

Hon, L. C., & Grunig, J. E. (1999). *Measuring relationships in public relations*. Retrieved from www.instituteforpr.org/wp-content/uploads/Guidelines_Measuring_Relationships.pdf

Hustak, A. (2004, January 4). A gentle and thoughtful man: Journalist wrote, edited, widely-quoted Royal Bank Letter, *The Gazette*, D7. ProQuest.

International Communication Agency. (1978). Federal government's organization for conducting nation's public diplomacy. *Department of State Bulletin*, *78*. Retrieved from www.state.gov/wp-content/uploads/2019/06/1980-International-Communications-Agency-Report.pdf

Ipsos. (2019). *Ipsos public affairs Anholt Ipsos nation brands index (NBI)*. Retrieved from www.ipsos.com/sites/default/files/anholt-ipsos-nation-brands-index.pdf

Iriye, A. (1979). Culture and power: International relations as intercultural relations. *Diplomatic History*, *3*(2), 115–128. doi:10.1111/j.1467-7709.1979.tb00305.x

Jain, R., De Moya, M., & Molleda, J. (2014). State of international public relations research: Narrowing the knowledge gap about the practice across borders. *Public Relations Review*, *40*(3), 595–597. doi:10.1016/j.pubrev.2014.02.009

Johanson, J., & Vahlne, J. (2009). The Uppsala internationalization process model revisited: From liability of foreignness to liability of outsidership. *The Journal of International Business Studies*, *40*, 1411–1431.

Ki, E. (2015). Application of relationship management to public diplomacy. In G. J. Golan, S. Yang, & D. F. Kinsey (Eds.), *International public relations and public diplomacy* (pp. 93–108). New York, NY: Peter Lang.

Kingsley, R. (1967). The public diplomacy of U.S. business abroad: The experience of Latin America. *Journal of Inter-American Studies*, *9*(3), 413–428. doi:10.2307/164800

Kochhar, S. K., & Molleda, J. C. (2015). The evolving links between international public relations and corporate diplomacy. In G. J. Golan, S. Yang, & D. F. Kinsey (Eds.), *International public relations and public diplomacy* (pp. 51–71). New York, NY: Peter Lang.

Ledingham, J. A., & Bruning, S. D. (2000). *Public relations as relationship management: A relational approach to the study and practice of public relations*. Mahwah, NJ: Lawrence Erlbaum Associates, Ltd.

Leonard, M., Stead, C., & Smewing, C. (2002). *Public diplomacy*. London: The Foreign Policy Centre.

A lesson in diplomacy. (1823, September 1). *The Museum of Foreign Literature, Science, and Art (1822–1842)*, *3*(15), 224. ProQuest.

L'Etang, J. (1996). Public relations as diplomacy. In J. L'Etang & M. Pieczka (Eds.), *Critical perspectives in public relations* (pp. 14–34). London: International Thomson Business Press.

L'Etang, J. (2009). Public relations and diplomacy in a globalized world: An issue of public communication. *American Behavioral Scientist*, *53*(4), 607–626. doi:10.1177/0002764209347633

Lowes, M. (2002). *Indy dreams and urban nightmares: Speed merchants, spectacle, and the struggle over public space in the world-class city*. Toronto, Canada: University of Toronto Press.

Lundgren, E. F. (1974). *Organizational management: Systems and process*. San Francisco, CA: Canfield Press.

Malešević, S., & Pavasović Trošt, T. (2018, December 13). Nation-state and nationalism. In *The Blackwell encyclopedia of sociology*. Retrieved from doi. org/10.1002/9781405165518.wbeosn003.pub2

Marsden, M. (1994). The Royal Bank of Canada *Letter* as international educational tool. *Journal of American Culture*, *17*(4), 41–45. doi:10.1111/j.1542-734X.1994. t01-1-00041.x

Maxwell, R. (2007, September 27). *The place of arts and culture in Canadian foreign policy*. Paper prepared for the Canadian Conference of the Arts. Retrieved from http://ccarts.ca/wp-content/uploads/2009/01/PDS-BackgrounddocumentENGFINALgs27.09.07.pdf

McClory, J. (2017). *The soft power 30: A global ranking of soft power 2017*. Retrieved from https://softpower30.com/wp-content/uploads/2017/07/The-Soft-Power-30-Report-2017-Web-1.pdf

McClory, J., & Harvey, O. (2016). The soft power 30: Getting to grips with the measurement challenge. *Global Affairs*, *3*(2), 309–319. doi:10.1080/23340460. 2016.1239379

McDowall, D. (1993). *Quick to the frontier: Canada's Royal Bank*. Retrieved from www.rbc.com/history/celebrating-our-history/quick-to-the-frontier.html

Melissen, J. (2005). *The new diplomacy: Soft power in international relations*. New York, NY: Palgrave Macmillan.

Mitchell, J. M. (1986). *International cultural relations*. London: Allen and Unwin.

Mitchell, R. G. Jr., & Charmaz, K. (1996). Telling tales, writing stories: Postmodernist visions and realist images in ethnographic writing. *Journal of Contemporary Ethnography*, *25*(1), 144–166. doi:10.1177/089124196025001008

Mitra, R. (2012). The famine in British India: Quantification rhetoric and colonial disaster management. *Journal of Creative Commons*, *7*(1–2), 153–174. doi:10.1177/0973258613501066

Molleda, J. C., & Laskin, A. V. (2005). *Global, international, comparative and regional public relations knowledge from 1995-2005: A quantitative content analysis of academic and trade publications*. Retrieved from https://instituteforpr. org/wp-content/uploads/Int_PR_Knowledge.pdf

Moloney, K. (2006). *Rethinking public relations: PR propaganda and democracy* (2nd ed.). London: Routledge.

The Montreal Press Club announces the winners of 'Canada's Richest Essay Competition'. (2006, March 15). *Canada Newswire*, 1. ProQuest.

Mulcahy, K. V. (1999). Cultural diplomacy and the exchange programs: 1938–1978. *The Journal of Arts Management, Law and Society, 29*(1), 7–28. doi:10.1080/10632929909597282

Muscato, C. (2018). *Nation-state*. Retrieved from https://study.com/academy/lesson/nation-state-definition-examples-characteristics.html

Nisbett, M. (2013). New perspectives on instrumentalism: An empirical study of cultural diplomacy. *International Journal of Cultural Policy, 19*(5), 557–575. doi:10.1080/10286632.2012.704628

Nuri, M. (2017, April 12). *Applying Joseph Nye's concept of 'soft power'*. Retrieved from www.shine.cn/archive/opinion/foreign-perspectives/Applying-Joseph-Nyes-concept-of-soft-power/shdaily.shtml

Nye, J. (1990). *Bound to lead: The changing nature of American power*. New York, NY: Basic Books.

Nye, J. (2004). *Soft power: The means to success in world politics*. New York, NY: Public Affairs.

Nye, J. (2011). *The future of power*. New York, NY: Public Affairs.

Nye, J. (2017). *Soft power: The origins and political progress of a concept*. Retrieved from www.nature.com/articles/palcomms20178.pdf?origin=ppub

Parry, P. (2014). *Eisenhower: The public relations president*. Lanham, MD: Lexington Books.

Payne, J. (2009). Reflections on public diplomacy: People-to-people communication. *American Behavioral Scientist, 53*(4), 579–606. doi:10.1177/0002764209347632

Pimple, M. M. (2012). Business ethics and corporate social responsibility. *International Journal of Management Research and Review, 2*(5), 761–765.

Popper, K. (1959). *The logic of scientific discovery*. London: Hutchinson and Company.

Potter, E. (2009). *Branding Canada: Projecting Canada's soft power through public diplomacy*. Montreal, Canada: McGill-Queens University Press.

Ralston Saul, J. (1994). *Culture and foreign policy: Canada's foreign policy position papers*. Ottawa: Canada Communication Group.

RBC. (1943, December). India. *RBC Letter*. Retrieved from www.rbc.com/aboutus/letter/pdf/december1943.pdf

RBC. (1945, June). *Canada's government*. Retrieved from www.rbc.com/aboutus/letter/pdf/june1945.pdf

RBC. (1946, June). *International trade*. Retrieved from www.rbc.com/aboutus/letter/june1946.html

RBC. (1947, March). Representatives abroad. *RBC Letter, 28*(3). Retrieved from www.rbc.com/aboutus/letter/pdf/march1947.pdf

RBC. (1957, December). Preserving our freedom. *RBC Letter, 38*(12). Retrieved from www.rbc.com/aboutus/letter/pdf/december1957.pdf

RBC. (1974, September). The work ethic is not dead. *RBC Letter, 55*(9). Retrieved from www.rbc.com/aboutus/letter/pdf/september1974.pdf

RBC. (1984, May–June). Punishment and crime. *RBC Letter, 65*(3). Retrieved from www.rbc.com/aboutus/letter/pdf/may_jun1984.pdf

RBC. (1994, January–February). Royal Bank letter commemorative edition. *RBC Letter, 75*(1). Retrieved from www.rbc.com/aboutus/letter/pdf/jan_feb1994.pdf

RBC. (2002). *RBC letter moves online.* Retrieved from www.rbc.com/aboutus/letter/september2002.html

RBC. (2019a). *RBC letter.* Retrieved from www.rbc.com/aboutus/letter/history.html

RBC. (2019b). *Corporate profile.* Retrieved from www.rbc.com/aboutus/index.html

RBC. (2019c). *International business outside North America.* Retrieved from www.rbc.com/history/milestones-at-a-glance/international-business.html

RBC. (2019d). *RBC letter.* Retrieved from www.rbc.com/aboutus/letter/index.html

The relation of diplomacy to the development of international law, public and private. (1902). *The American Law Review (1866–1906), 36,* 160. ProQuest.

Richardson, Stuart. (1985, March 7). The Royal Bank Letter. Town of Mount Royal Weekly Post, pp. 4-5.

Rivera, T. (2015). *Distinguishing cultural relations from cultural diplomacy: The British Council's relationship with her majesty's government.* Retrieved from www.uscpublicdiplomacy.org/sites/uscpublicdiplomacy.org/files/useruploads/u33041/Distinguishing%20Cultural%20Relations%20From%20Cultural%20Diplomacy%20-%20Full%20Version%20(1).pdf

Royal Bank Letter Commends Bills. (1934, July 5). *The Globe (1844–1936).*

Samuilova, I. (2004, March 11–12). *Public relations in Bulgaria – From the chaos of the transition to the horizons of globalization.* Paper presented to the 7th International Public Relations Researcher's Conference, Miami, FL.

Saner, R., & Yui, L. (2003, January). *International economic diplomacy: Mutations in post-modern times.* Discussion paper presented at Netherlands Institute of International Relations, Clingendael, Netherlands. Retrieved from www.diplomacydialogue.org/images/files/20030109-DP-DSP.pdf

Saner, R., Yiu, L., & Søndergaard, M. (2000). Business diplomacy management: A core competency for global companies. *The Academy of Management Executive, 14*(1), 80–92.

Scherer, A. G., & Palazzo, G. (2007). Toward a political conception of corporate responsibility: Business and society seen from a Habermasian perspective. *Academy of Management Review, 32*(4), 1096–1120. doi:10.5465/amr.2007.26585837

Senne, L., & Moore, S. (2015). Bismarck, propaganda and public relations. *Public Relations Review, 41*(3), 326–334. doi:10.1016/j.pubrev.2015.04.001

Signitzer, B. (2008). Public relations and public diplomacy: Some conceptual explorations. In A. Zerfaß, A. A. van Ruler, & K. Sriramesh (Eds.), *Public relations research: European and international perspectives and innovations* (pp. 205–218). Wiesbaden, Germany: VS Verlag for the Social Sciences.

Signitzer, B., & Coombs, T. (1992). Public relations and public diplomacy: Conceptual convergences. *Public Relations Review, 18*(2), 137–147. doi:10.1016/0363-8111(92)90005-J

Signitzer, B., & Wamser, C. (2006). Public diplomacy: A special governmental public relations function. In C. Botan & V. Hazleton (Eds.), *Public relations theory II* (pp. 435–464). Mahwah, NJ: Lawrence Erlbaum Associates.

Snow, N. (2005). U.S. public diplomacy: Its history, problems, and promise. In G. S. Jowett & V. O'Donnell (Eds.), *Readings in propaganda: New and classic essays* (pp. 225–241). Thousand Oaks, CA: Sage.

Snow, N. (2009). Rethinking public diplomacy. In N. Snow & P. M. Taylor (Eds.), *Routledge handbook of public diplomacy* (pp. 3–11). New York, NY: Routledge.

Snow, N. (2015). Public diplomacy and public relations: Will the twain ever meet? In G. J. Golan, S. Yang, & D. F. Kinsey (Eds.), *International public relations and public diplomacy* (pp. 73–90). New York, NY: Peter Lang.

Tye, L. (1998). *The father of spin: Edward L. Bernays and the birth of public relations*. New York, NY: Crown.

Van Dyke, M. A., & Verčič, D. (2009). Public relations, public diplomacy and strategic communication: An international model of conceptual convergence. In K. Sriramesh & D. Verčič (Eds.), *Global public relations handbook: Theory, research and practice* (pp. 822–842). New York, NY: Routledge.

van Ham, P. (2008). Place branding: The state of the art. *The Annals of the American Academy of Political and Social Science, 616*(1), 126–149. doi:10.1177/0002716207312274

Vanc, A., & Fitzpatrick, K. (2016). Scope and status of public diplomacy research by public relations scholars, 1990–2014. *Public Relations Review, 42*(3), 432–440. doi:10.1016/j.pubrev.2015.07.012

von Flotow, L. (2007). Telling Canada's story in German: Using cultural diplomacy to achieve soft power. In L. von Flotow & R. M. Nischik (Eds.), *Translating Canada* (pp. 9–26). Ottawa, Canada: University of Ottawa Press.

Walton, J. (1992). Making the theoretical case. In C. C. Ragin & H. S. Becker (Eds.), *What is a case? Exploring the foundations of social inquiry* (pp. 121–137). New York, NY: Cambridge University Press.

Wang, J. (2006a). Public diplomacy and global business. *Journal of Business Strategy, 27*(3), 41–49. doi:10.1108/02756660610663826

Wang, J. (2006b). Managing national reputation and international relations in the global era: Public diplomacy revisited. *Public Relations Review, 32*(2), 91–96. doi.org/10.1016/j.pubrev.2005.12.001

Weber, M. (1922). *Economy and society*. Los Angeles, CA: University of California Press.

Welch, J. M. (1991). Free bank letters as sources of economic and financial information. *Journal of Business and Finance Librarianship, 1*(2), 5–17. doi:10.1300/J109v01n02_02

Whitaker and Company. (1847). *British diplomacy in the River Plate* [Pamphlet]. London. Retrieved from www.jstor.org.libproxy.mtroyal.ca/stable/60234116

White, C. (2015). Exploring the role of private-sector corporations in public diplomacy. *Public Relations Inquiry, 4*(3), 305–321. doi:10.1177/2046147X15614883

Wilcox, D., Ault, P. H., Agee, W. K., & Cameron, G. T. (2001). *Essentials of public relations*. New York, NY: Longman.

Wingrove, J., & Martin, P. (2019, March 28). *China's canola ban adds to Trudeau's woes in bitter Huawei feud*. Retrieved from www.msn.com/en-ca/money/topstories/chinas-canola-ban-adds-to-trudeaus-woes-in-bitter-huawei-feud/ar-BBVk2Sx

Yang, A., Taylor, M., & Saffer, A. (2016). Ethical convergence, divergence or communitas? An examination of public relations and journalism codes of ethics. *Public Relations Review, 42*(1), 146–160. doi:10.1016/j.pubrev.2015.08.001

Yun, S. H. (2009). Towards public relations theory-based study of public diplomacy: Testing the applicability of the excellence study. *Journal of Public Relations Research, 18*(4), 287–312. doi:10.1207/s1532754xjprr1804_1

Yun, S. H., & Toth, E. (2009). Future sociological public diplomacy and the role of public relations: Evolution of public diplomacy. *American Behavioral Scientist, 53*(4), 493–503.

Zaharna, R. S. (2009). *Battles to bridges: US strategic communication and public diplomacy after 9/11*. London: Palgrave Macmillan.

Zartman, I. (2016). Diplomacy and negotiation. In C. M. Constantinou, P. Kerr, & P. Sharp (Eds.), *The SAGE handbook of diplomacy* (pp. 207–219). London: SAGE Publications Ltd. doi:10.4135/9781473957930.n18

Index

For Product Safety Concerns and Information please contact our EU
representative GPSR@taylorandfrancis.com
Taylor & Francis Verlag GmbH, Kaufingerstraße 24, 80331 München, Germany